Kathy Weingarten
Michele Bograd
Editors

Reflections on Feminist Family Therapy Training

Pre-publication
REVIEWS,
COMMENTARIES,
EVALUATIONS . . .

"**T**hird World and European voices are well-represented, jarring the North American reader out of complacency. Narrative and social constructivist theories come alive as applied to personally lived situations. Relationships with institutions, colleagues, and trainees all become material for experiential learning.

There are a wealth of specific experiential exercises and extensive bibliographies. Those new to a feminist perspective on family therapy will find their eyes widened: experienced trainers will become immersed in the subjective dialogue."

Kathleen McGuire, PhD
Center for the Study of Women in Society
University of Oregon, Eugene

"**T**his book offers more than its title promises! It provides a lucid picture of the evolution of the role of feminism in the family therapy field since 1978, along with a lot of good information about how to integrate feminism into family therapy training. Nothing could serve the feminist cause better than the intelligence, courage, and humanity demonstrated by the contributors to this volume.

What I appreciate most about this book is that despite its largely narrative style and practical suggestions it does not sacrifice theoretical and clinical depth. It is hard to point to any one chapter as having more merit than another. Each is interesting to read and well documented. The majority of chapters reflect the experience and ideas of trainers in a variety of contexts, such as public and private training institutions and graduate social work programs. The lone chapter that presents the student perspective was authored by Pilar Hernandez, a member of a non-dominant culture. Her chapter eloquently illustrates the need to consider both culture and gender in family therapy training. Rosmarie Welter-Enderlin's chapter, a summary of a survey she conducted among twelve family therapy trainers in six central European countries, points to the effect of sociocultural differences in gender-informed family therapy training.

AAMFT would do well to make this volume required reading for supervisees and supervisors."

Eve Lipchik, MSW
Vice-President
ICF Consultants, Inc.
Milwaukee, WI

More pre-publication
REVIEWS, COMMENTARIES, EVALUATIONS . . .

"**I** read Weingarten and Bograd's manuscript *Reflections on Feminist Family Therapy Training* en route to the 1996 American Family Therapy Academy meeting. At the AFTA meeting, someone asked me who had mentored me through the labyrinth of gaining tenure, teaching, publishing, and clinical practice in a large university. It was a shock to realize that I never had a female mentor–some helpful males along the way did offer support, but many did everything they could to undermine my membership in the "all boys' department." I wish that Weingarten and Bograd's volume had been available to me twenty years ago. I would not have felt so isolated and inadequate. These articles will be enormously helpful not only to women but also to members of other non-dominant groups (such as people of color, gays, and lesbians) struggling with the traditional power structures of established professional institutions and organizations."

Barbara F. Okun, PhD
Professor and Co-Clinical Coordinator
Department of Counseling Psychology
Northeastern University
Boston, MA

The Haworth Press, Inc.

Reflections on Feminist Family Therapy Training

Reflections on Feminist Family Therapy Training

Kathy Weingarten
Michele Bograd
Editors

The Haworth Press, Inc.
New York · London

Reflections on Feminist Family Therapy Training has also been published as *Journal of Feminist Family Therapy,* Volume 8, Number 2 1996.

The development, preparation, and publication of this work has been undertaken with great care. However, the publisher, employees, editors, and agents of The Haworth Press and all imprints of The Haworth Press, Inc., including The Haworth Medical Press and Pharmaceutical Products Press, are not responsible for any errors contained herein or for consequences that may ensue from use of materials or information contained in this work. Opinions expressed by the author(s) are not necessarily those of The Haworth Press, Inc.

The Haworth Press, Inc., 10 Alice Street, Binghamton, NY 13904-1580 USA

Library of Congress Cataloging-in-Publication Data

Reflections on feminist family therapy training / Kathy Weingarten, Michele Bograd, editors.
    p. cm.
Includes bibliographical references and index.
ISBN 0-7890-0002-4 (alk. paper)
    1. Feminist therapy–Study and teaching. 2. Family psychotherapy–Study and teaching. 3. Women psychotherapists–Training of. I. Weingarten, Kathy. II. Bograd, Michele Louise, 1952- .
RC489.F45R44 1996
616.89'156–dc20   96-30446
                                                       CIP

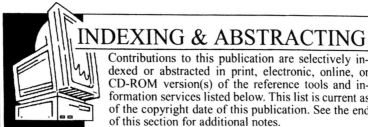

INDEXING & ABSTRACTING

Contributions to this publication are selectively indexed or abstracted in print, electronic, online, or CD-ROM version(s) of the reference tools and information services listed below. This list is current as of the copyright date of this publication. See the end of this section for additional notes.

- *Abstracts of Research in Pastoral Care & Counseling,* Loyola College, 7135 Minstrel Way, Suite 101, Columbia, MD 21045

- *Alternative Press Index,* Alternative Press Center, Inc., P.O. Box 33109, Baltimore, MD 21218-0401

- *Applied Social Science Index & Abstracts (ASSIA) (Online: ASSI via Data-Star) (CDRom: ASSIA Plus),* Bowker-Saur Limited, Maypole House, Maypole Road, East Grinstead, West Sussex RH19 1HH, England

- *CNPIEC Reference Guide: Chinese National Directory of Foreign Periodicals,* P.O. Box 88, Beijing, People's Republic of China

- *Family Studies Database (online and CD/ROM),* Peters Technology Transfer, 306 East Baltimore Pike, 2nd Floor, Media, PA 19063

- *Family Violence & Sexual Assault Bulletin,* Family Violence & Sexual Assault Institute, 1310 Clinic Drive, Tyler, TX 75701

- *Feminist Periodicals: A Current Listing of Contents,* Women's Studies Librarian-at-Large, 728 State Street, 430 Memorial Library, Madison, WI 53706

(continued)

- *IBZ International Bibliography of Periodical Literature,* Zeller Verlag GmbH & Co., P.O.B. 1949, D-49009 Osnabruck, Germany

- *Index to Periodical Articles Related to Law,* University of Texas, 727 East 26th Street, Austin, TX 78705

- *INTERNET ACCESS (& additional networks) Bulletin Board for Libraries ("BUBL"), coverage of information resources on INTERNET, JANET, and other networks.*
  - JANET X.29: UK.AC.BATH.BUBL or 00006012101300
  - TELNET: BUBL.BATH.AC.UK or 138.38.32.45 login 'bubl'
  - Gopher: BUBL.BATH.AC.UK (138.32.32.45). Port 7070
  - World Wide Web: http: / / www.bubl.bath.ac.uk./BUBL/ home.html
  - NISSWAIS: telnetniss.ac.uk (for the NISS gateway)
  The Andersonian Library, Curran Building, 101 St. James Road, Glasgow G4 ONS, Scotland

- *Mental Health Abstracts (online through DIALOG),* IFI/Plenum Data Company, 3202 Kirkwood Highway, Wilmington, DE 19808

- *Social Work Abstracts,* National Association of Social Workers, 750 First Street NW, 8th Floor, Washington, DC 20002

- *Studies on Women Abstracts,* Carfax Publishing Company, P.O. Box 25, Abingdon, Oxfordshire OX14 3UE, United Kingdom

- *Violence and Abuse Abstracts: A Review of Current Literature on Interpersonal Violence (VAA),* Sage Publications, Inc., 2455 Teller Road, Newbury Park, CA 91320

- *Women Studies Abstracts,* Rush Publishing Company, P.O. Box 1, Rush, NY 14543

(continued)

SPECIAL BIBLIOGRAPHIC NOTES

related to special journal issues (separates)
and indexing/abstracting

☐ indexing/abstracting services in this list will also cover material in any "separate" that is co-published simultaneously with Haworth's special thematic journal issue or DocuSerial. Indexing/abstracting usually covers material at the article/chapter level.

☐ monographic co-editions are intended for either non-subscribers or libraries which intend to purchase a second copy for their circulating collections.

☐ monographic co-editions are reported to all jobbers/wholesalers/approval plans. The source journal is listed as the "series" to assist the prevention of duplicate purchasing in the same manner utilized for books-in-series.

☐ to facilitate user/access services all indexing/abstracting services are encouraged to utilize the co-indexing entry note indicated at the bottom of the first page of each article/chapter/contribution.

☐ this is intended to assist a library user of any reference tool (whether print, electronic, online, or CD-ROM) to locate the monographic version if the library has purchased this version but not a subscription to the source journal.

☐ individual articles/chapters in any Haworth publication are also available through the Haworth Document Delivery Services (HDDS).

Reflections on Feminist Family Therapy Training

CONTENTS

ABOUT THE EDITORS

Kathy Weingarten, PhD, is Co-Director of the Program in Narrative Approaches to Therapy at the Family Institute of Cambridge and an Assistant Professor of Psychology at Harvard Medical School. She has a private practice in Newton. She is the author of *The Mother's Voice: Strengthening Intimacy in Families* (Harcourt Brace, 1994) and the editor of *Cultural Resistance: Challenging Beliefs About Men, Women, and Therapy* (The Haworth Press, Inc., 1995). She is on the Board of the American Family Therapy Academy and on the editorial boards of the *Journal of Feminist Family Therapy* and *Family Process*. In 1995, she was the co-recipient of the Psychotherapy with Women award of Division 35 of the American Psychological Association. Dr. Weingarten's areas of specialization include the social construction of mothers, parent-adolescent interaction, intimacy, and narrative therapy.

Michele Bograd, PhD, is a psychologist in private practice in Arlington, Massachusetts, and a faculty member of the Family Institute of Cambridge in Watertown, Massachusetts. She has also taught and supervised family therapists at the Kantor Family Institute in Somerville, Massachusetts, and at Harvard Medical School. A frequent participant in state and national conferences and workshops, her research interests include the dynamics of feminist therapy, feminist approaches for treating men in family therapy, violence against women, gender and power, and the cultural biases in therapy. She is the co-editor of *Feminist Perspectives on Wife Abuse* (Sage, 1988) and the editor of *Feminist Approaches to Treating Men in Family Therapy* (The Haworth Press, Inc., 1990). A contributing editor of *Family Therapy Networker* and a member of the editorial board of the *Journal of Feminist Family Therapy*, Dr. Bograd is a member of the American Family Therapy Academy, the American Association of Marriage and Family Therapy, and the American Psychological Association.

Among Ourselves:
Creating Opportunities for Speaking About the Teaching of Feminist Family Therapy

Kathy Weingarten
Michele Bograd

The idea for this volume took form on an airplane ride that we took from an American Family Therapy Academy meeting in Santa Fe to Boston. We had more uninterrupted time together than we ever get and we began to feel quite giddy with the happiness of the opportunity. We were good friends already, and like schoolgirls confiding in each other, our speaking about our professional lives went deeper and deeper into concerns we had spoken of before but without the richness and multilayeredness of this special conversation.

Eventually, perhaps over Illinois, we began talking about ourselves as feminists and the ways we feel supported and constrained by the various institutional contexts and collegial relationships that

Kathy Weingarten, PhD, is Co-Director of the Program in Narrative Therapies, The Family Institute of Cambridge and Michele Bograd, PhD, is in private practice in Arlington, MA.

Address correspondence to Kathy Weingarten, 82 Homer Street, Newton Centre, MA 02159.

[Haworth co-indexing entry note]: "Among Ourselves: Creating Opportunities for Speaking About the Teaching of Feminist Family Therapy." Weingarten, Kathy, and Michele Bograd. Co-published simultaneously in *Journal of Feminist Family Therapy* (The Haworth Press, Inc.) Vol. 8, No. 2, 1996, pp. 1-5; and: *Reflections on Feminist Family Therapy Training* (ed: Kathy Weingarten, and Michele Bograd) The Haworth Press, Inc., 1996, pp. 1-5. Single or multiple copies of this article are available from The Haworth Document Delivery Service [1-800-342-9678, 9:00 a.m. - 5:00 p.m. (EST). E-mail address: getinfo@haworth.com].

we are in—one of which, at the Family Institute of Cambridge, we share. We opened up to each other about what it was like for us, holding a feminist position, to speak out (or not) in faculty meetings, to teach students, and to collaborate with colleagues in a context that defines itself as a nonsexist, liberal family therapy center. We acknowledged to each other that it was a relief to name and share aspects of our more private and personal experiences and to describe the vulnerabilities and struggles in a context that, for the most part, seemed accepting of our feminist sensibilities.

About an hour from Boston we began reflecting on the differences between this conversation and many others we had shared, all undertaken in the spirit of complete frankness. With great curiosity, we began to speculate on what factors permitted us to enter previously unspoken territory. We both agreed that a sense of isolation was operative. It was as if being suspended in midair provided us protection. But from what? Our best guesses included the embarrassment of admitting that as senior feminist family therapists we struggle with gaps between our beliefs and practices, the risks of exposing some of the inner workings of the institutions with which we are each affiliated, and the hurt or defensive reactions of colleagues who believe they share our politics.

As we were landing, we hatched an idea to explore these issues with other feminist colleagues. We wanted to bring a personal dimension into the public arena. We realized, as feminists constantly rediscover, that our dilemmas were due less to our individual confusions than to the inevitable tensions facing any feminist family therapy teacher. We were eager to hear from other trainers how, in the privacy of their own work and growth, they had developed ideas and strategies about tolerating, working with, and resolving these tensions in their specific institutional contexts. We decided to propose coediting a publication which would examine the subjective experiences of feminist family therapy teachers.

We were still in the air. Two weeks later, we met to pursue our project. By that time, we had done a review of the literature on feminist family therapy training. We found, in general, that the understandable focus of groundbreaking pieces (see, for example, Ault-Riche, 1988; Avis, 1989a, 1989b; Sirles, 1994; Wheeler, Avis, Miller & Chaney, 1989) was on curriculum development, on creating bibliographies, and on the reactions and struggles of male and female students. Somehow, the voices of the woman trainers themselves were sidelined.

In thinking about shaping this volume, we speculated about what might influence the subjective experiences of feminist family therapy teachers. Does where one teaches, be it in a private institute or an academic setting, make a difference? How do North American contexts differ from European ones? How does the relative position of the trainer, such as national prominence or tenure status, promote or inhibit her freedom to practice openly in an explicitly feminist manner? How welcoming is the training context to feminism and/or family therapy? How is diversity integrated into a feminist family therapy training experience?

With these questions in mind, we solicited articles from our contributors with an invitation that included the following ideas:

> We have been curious about the experiences of other feminist family therapists: how do others implement a feminist perspective in their teaching? What special dilemmas or opportunities face others in various work contexts, such as providing training in a mainstream academic institution, a training institute, or as a free agent? What strategies have been helpful to others and what teaching exercises or approaches feel most creative?
>
> We would like the pieces to be personal, provocative, and practical—revealing dilemmas, suggesting strategies for dealing with particular institutional contexts, describing useful exercises or approaches to the material, sharing what worked and what backfired. In short, we are interested in the wisdom you have developed over the years. In this spirit, the article need not be formal nor include a review of the literature. We'd like the piece to be grounded in your experience.

In response to this invitation, the following authors contributed to our issue: Cheryl Rampage, a leader in the North American feminist family therapy movement and senior faculty member at the Chicago Family Institute; N. Norma Akamatsu (adjunct faculty), Kathryn Basham (full-time faculty) and Mary Olson (adjunct faculty), three thoughtful teachers at the Smith School for Social Work;

Pilar Hernandez, an energetic Colombian graduate student in the feminist informed family therapy training program at the University of Massachusetts in Amherst; and Rosmarie Welter-Enderlin, a prominent European feminist family therapist, who teaches at the Meilen/Zurich Institute in Switzerland. We asked Judith Myers Avis, eminent in the North American feminist family therapy movement and a faculty member in a Canadian university, to respond to these papers with an eye to both the subjective experiences of the authors and to the future directions of feminist family therapy training as suggested by these articles.

We found these articles interesting and engaging. We were struck both by what we learned and what we still wanted to hear. The voices of the authors felt vivid and self-revealing in some of the pieces, somewhat more abstract or distant in others. Was this due to the personal preferences of the authors and/or were they writing under some of the very constraints that led us to contemplate this publication in the first place? Our curiosity was piqued as we read these important contributions about what more we could learn about the intimate, exhilarating and sometimes trying experiences of being among those who risk explicitly identifying as feminist family therapists? As we wondered why our authors had taken various degrees of personal risk in their writing, we were left facing the question ourselves: what had kept us from writing our own self-revealing piece?

Perhaps our goal of detailing feminist family therapists' experiences needs to proceed along with an effort to create safe and protected places for self-revelation and connection. We hope that this volume will be a start in creating such a space, and we hope that it will encourage more writing and speaking about the passions and vulnerabilities of pursuing a feminist family therapy agenda in training contexts.

REFERENCES

Ault-Riche, M. (1988). Teaching an integrated model of family therapy: Women as students, women as supervisors. In L. Braverman (Ed.), *Women, feminism and family therapy.* New York: The Haworth Press, Inc.

Avis, J.M. (1989a). Reference guide to feminism and family therapy. *Journal of Feminist Family Therapy, 1* (1), 94-100.

Avis, J.M. (1989b). Integrating gender into the family therapy curriculum. *Journal of Feminist Family Therapy, 1* (2), 3-26.

Sirles, E. (1994). Teaching feminist family therapy: Practicing what we preach. *Journal of Feminist Family Therapy, 6* (1), 1-26.

Wheeler, D., Avis, J.M., Miller, L. & Chaney, S. (1989). Rethinking family therapy training and supervision: A feminist model. In M. McGoldrick, C.M. Anderson & F. Walsh (Eds.), *Women in families: A framework for family therapy* (pp. 135-151). New York: W.W. Norton & Co.

On Being a Feminist Trainer
in an Independent Institute

Cheryl Rampage

SUMMARY. This paper examines the challenges of being a feminist in an institutional setting which is not itself feminist in orientation. Dilemmas around curriculum, supervision, and relationships with both trainees and colleagues are explored. Specific suggestions are offered for how to manage some of the complexities of working within an institutional setting. *[Article copies available from The Haworth Document Delivery Service: 1-800-342-9678. E-mail address: getinfo@haworth.com]*

For almost my entire professional life, I have been associated with free-standing institutes involved in the training of family therapists. Reconciling family therapy and feminism has always been a fight for me, and I don't like to fight alone. By nature I am a collaborator, and I have always done my best work when functioning as part of a collective. I think better when I develop my ideas in conversation with others. The ideas themselves come out more nuanced and more complex. Without question, I am also braver and more willing to challenge conventional wisdom or strong opposition of any kind when I am in the company of sympathetic souls. Expanding the scope and influence of family therapy through my

Cheryl Rampage, PhD, is Director of Graduate Education, The Family Institute, 618 Library Place, Evanston, IL 60201.

[Haworth co-indexing entry note]: "On Being a Feminist Trainer in an Independent Institute." Rampage, Cheryl. Co-published simultaneously in *Journal of Feminist Family Therapy* (The Haworth Press, Inc.) Vol. 8, No. 2, 1996, pp. 7-19; and: *Reflections on Feminist Family Therapy Training* (ed: Kathy Weingarten, and Michele Bograd) The Haworth Press, Inc., 1996, pp. 7-19. Single or multiple copies of this article are available from The Haworth Document Delivery Service [1-800-342-9678, 9:00 a.m. - 5:00 p.m. (EST). E-mail address: getinfo@haworth.com].

involvement in training others has been one of my professional missions; the other has been to implore, argue, nag and cajole family therapy to recognize the significance of gender as a clinical variable.

During the course of the past sixteen years, I have been on the faculty of three free-standing institutes involved in the training of family therapists: The Galveston Family Institute, The Women's Institute for Life Studies, and the Family Institute at Northwestern University. These experiences form the basis for the remarks I will offer in this paper.

By way of introduction, the Galveston Family Institute (GFI) provides clinical services and training to professional therapists interested in learning about the unique systemic methods of its founders, the late Harry Goolishian and Harlene Anderson. I was a student at GFI in 1979-81, and a member of its adjunct faculty from 1981-1984. The Women's Institute for Life Studies (WILS) was formed by myself and three other feminist therapists who had been students at GFI and found it inhospitable to our questions about gender. WILS had the mission of providing educational activities to women, both therapists and non-therapists, that would enhance their feminism. I was a founding faculty member of WILS, which existed from 1984 until 1990. Since 1989 I have been a full-time staff member of the Family Institute at Northwestern University (FI), formerly known as the Family Institute of Chicago. Founded in 1968, the mission of FI is to strengthen and heal families through clinical practice and clinical training. I am one of eight staff-directors at FI, and am responsible for all graduate level programming, including a master's degree program in marital and family therapy offered through our affiliation with Northwestern.

Like most feminist therapists of my generation, my feminism preceded the attainment of my professional credentials by many years. Throughout graduate school I alternately struggled to keep my gender values separate from my professional responsibilities, as my professors instructed, and attempted to integrate them, which usually resulted in raised eyebrows and lower grades. It wasn't until I read Rachel Hare-Mustin's landmark paper on feminism and family therapy (1978) that I first felt support for my desire to integrate my politics and my practice. By then I was in Texas, the home of the Kilgore ("beauty knows no pain") Rangerettes, the Dallas Cowgirls, and kicker bars. At first glance, not a friendly environment for a feminist.

FEELING OUT OF CONTEXT

Still, on the theory that it is best to bloom where you are planted, I sought out opportunities to extend my training as a family therapist. Harry Goolishian was just forming the Galveston Family Institute with George Pulliam, Harlene Anderson, and Paul Dell. I spent two years with Harry and company, immersed both clinically and conceptually in expanding my thinking on systemic family therapy. I learned a great deal at GFI, but I also kept bumping up against the faculty's gender blindness. It wasn't that gender didn't get observed at GFI, but it was not, at least in those years, regarded as clinically meaningful.

Through the happy circumstance that GFI was located 50 miles from my home, I fell into the opportunity to carpool for two hours at a time with a fellow student in the training program, Thelma Jean Goodrich. In Thelma Jean I found a kindred spirit, someone who appreciated the same ideas and stumbled over the same difficulties as I did. Throughout that training year we rode up and down the freeway, discussing our fascination and misgivings regarding family therapy, GFI style. During the second year we found a few more women whose thoughts mirrored ours, and we began to meet for dinner at the end of the training day.

During the following two years I had a somewhat schizophrenic identity. I became an adjunct faculty member at GFI, and did some supervision in their training program, even as I continued to meet with my cohort of women trainees to read and discuss cases. Eventually, I realized that I had no voice at GFI, that my ideas were not well-received and that every time I mentioned the word *gender*, people's eyes glazed over. On the other hand, in my informal support group, I felt emboldened to be clear and forthright about my developing ideas regarding the role of gender, particularly in marital therapy.

BIRTHING AN INSTITUTE

How does an institute get started? Often, I suspect, in the same unplanned, haphazard, hesitant way that WILS began. First we were just a few women meeting at restaurants and sharing our reactions to other peoples' ideas. After a while, we began meeting at each other's offices, so as not to be disturbed by the sound of rattling dishes. From discussing the readings assigned in the GFI training program, it seemed like a small step to read things that one or more of us found intriguing. Eventually, with a courage that came more from zeal than from substance, we decided actually to offer *our* ideas to the public through workshops at local conferences. When that didn't bring the world to an end, it seemed that the logical next step was to form our own institute, where we could control the agenda. We discovered that forming an institute can be as simple and homespun as developing a mission statement and printing up a brochure with a few workshop offerings.

WILS didn't have the exclusive purpose of training family therapists, but as a matter of fact, many of our participants were trained as therapists and many of our offerings focused on the effect of patriarchy on the family in one form or another. It was strictly a shoestring operation, with the four of us providing the seed money and doing all of the grunt work, along with being the main presenters and teachers. In the best feminist tradition, there was no hierarchy. There wasn't a great deal of structure, either. There *was* a tremendous amount of energy and solidarity, encouragement for the expression and elaboration of each new, delicate, half-formed thought, and agreement about the role of gender in family life. Through the work with my WILS colleagues, it became clear to me that an examination of the relationship between gender and power in family life forms the conceptual basis of all feminist family therapy and that methodological differences between feminist therapists reflect the varieties of our clinical training experiences.

A serendipitous outcome of our penchant for presenting on gender in far-flung places ("missionary work," we called it) was that we came to the attention of Susan Munro at W.W. Norton who suggested to us that we write a book about the practice of feminist therapy. There is no question in my mind that none of us would ever have written this book alone. To have such controversial ideas exposed so publicly, to face the reactions that we were sure would be coming, would not have been tolerable. But, group psychology being what it is, it didn't seem so scary to be one of *four* women calling family therapy to task.

For the next several years we wrote the book as we continued to offer workshops, retreats, and consultation groups through WILS (and had full-time jobs and families, crises, and daily obligations). WILS provided the context for us to work together on understanding gender as a clinically meaningful concept. I have never felt so understood, so accepted, or so productive.

CHANGING CONTEXTS

However, even WILS was not enough to make me feel permanently at home in Texas. When my husband and I decided to return to our native Chicago, I immediately contacted Bill Pinsof at the Family Institute. I knew that FI was the biggest show in town, and had trained most of the family therapists in the Chicago area. Bill hired me to set up a master's degree program that FI was offering in collaboration with Northwestern University. I became the Director of Graduate Education, one of the eight directors responsible for the day-to-day management of the Institute. I am just ending my sixth year in that position.

I came to FI fresh on the heels of the successful publication of *Feminist Family Therapy: A Casebook*, coauthored with my colleagues from WILS, Thelma Jean Goodrich, Barbara Ellman, and Kris Halstead (1988). My reputation as a feminist preceded me to Chicago, and I chose to underscore that identity by doing a colloquium on the topic of gender issues in family therapy while I was interviewing for the position. As I reflect back on it, I think that I decided to be very pointed about my concerns regarding gender to prevent myself from being co-opted by yet another system in which gender had never been considered as relevant. During the interview process, more than one staff member politely asked me what I thought I might be interested in *after* feminism. I clearly understood that I was hired *in spite* of my interest in gender.

Being a feminist at the Family Institute is very different from being a feminist at GFI or WILS. At GFI I never had a position of influence, so my interest in feminism was not a threat to the prevailing order. At WILS my feminist voice was part of a chorus of such voices; I was continually emboldened and my ideas sharpened by being embedded in such a context. At FI my comments were a constant challenge to the prevailing order, a position which made for considerable discomfort for me, and, at times, for others on the staff as well.

In November of my first year at the Institute, I was asked to be the featured speaker at the fall faculty dinner, the main social and intellectual event of the year for the 50 or so adjunct faculty members of FI, as well as clinical staff. Again, I prepared a talk on my current thinking about the gender dilemmas contained in contemporary marriages. Just before I began speaking, as I looked over the sea of faces, almost all unfamiliar to me, I was seized with anxiety. Never was I more acutely aware of missing my colleagues from WILS. I think I even remarked out loud that I was going to pretend that I was one of four speakers at the podium, a Greek chorus of feminists. A woman in the audience smiled; our eyes met. I recognized a sympathetic soul, and with that for courage I began to speak.

Reaction to the talk was mixed. The women in the audience were largely very supportive and let me know that they thought it was about time that the Institute got into the 20th century. The men had a more varied reaction, ranging from very positive to enraged. One member of the audience was so furious at me that he literally could not form a coherent question. Most of the men were polite, if not very enthusiastic. This was consistent with the reactions I had been receiving to feminist presentations for years, so I considered it fairly normal. The next day one of my male colleagues suggested that I might want to think about my need to develop clinical referral sources in Chicago, and that he had heard a couple of men saying after the talk that they would certainly never refer a couple to me for treatment, given my obvious prejudice against men. At that moment I became aware of the power of the system to silence my voice, not by public censure, but by gentle suggestions that my politics would impact my livelihood.

I was quickly labeled the "resident expert" on gender at the

Institute, a token position of little honor. In those years, there was considerable tension around the question of gender between the staff, who were mostly male, and the trainees, who were mostly female. Very soon after my arrival, I started hearing from the female trainees that they were relieved that there was finally a woman at the Institute with the power to challenge the system around gender. In classes and case conferences I could feel the eyes of the women on me whenever the issue of gender came up (or should have been brought up). I became aware of feeling an enormous responsibility to speak clearly to the gender biases contained in my colleagues' diagnostic formulations or treatment strategies as well as those contained in the assigned readings and the clinical videotapes. I felt that I had a constituency in those women that I was honor-bound to represent well.

This sense of duty created an enormous bind as well, because I was *not* a trainee, but a staff member, and I risked being inducted into a collusion with the trainees against the staff. This pull to become triangulated has been one of the most challenging dilemmas associated with being at FI. During my own training experience, I had longed for a mentoring relationship in which my concerns about gender could be articulated and validated by a more senior, respected person. Like most feminists of my generation, I found that my longing went unfulfilled. There simply weren't enough senior women around, and those that there were tended to be unmoved by, and often even antipathetic to, feminism. I carried within me a strong desire to provide for younger women what I myself had wished for: a sympathetic ear and a supportive, affirming voice.

In practice, it turned out to be relatively easier to be a mentor in the privacy of the supervision room than the more public forum of the classroom. In supervision I could consult with a trainee on whether her reactions to a lecturer were valid, and, if so, worth fighting over. I could coach her on how to confront a supervisor or lecturer about some example of sexist behavior and empower her to defend her own ideas. In the classroom I had to deal with the potential for triangling between myself, the trainee, and the lecturer, as well as the politics of criticizing a colleague in front of trainees.

Whenever possible, I learned to encourage the trainee to voice her own challenge to the lecturer, rather than do it for her.

BRINGING GENDER TO SUPERVISION

In some respects, this mentoring function has been the most rewarding of all my experiences at FI. Early on, women started requesting me as a supervisor and I developed relationships with trainees in which the topic of gender was an explicit part of the agenda. In supervision, they would present the gender dilemmas they experienced in the clinical work and would ask for help analyzing their biases, their politics, and their clinical interventions.

Over the years, I have kept up with the small literature on feminist training in family therapy and I have incorporated some specific techniques into my supervision. One of the most useful tools I have found is the use of the trainee's genogram to discuss the gender myths, beliefs, and roles in their families of origin. Most of my trainees start out supervision with a fairly strong sense of the social inequities between men and women and equally strong feelings that they want to be involved in empowering their women clients. What they lack are the skills to empower women who are confused, frightened, unwilling, or unable to insist on having their voices heard. Also, of course, it is a delicate matter to empower a woman in heterosexual couples' treatment without triggering resistance in her partner. By closely examining their own genograms to learn more about how gender beliefs have been learned and modified, trainees discover ways to assist their clients in the same process.

This use of the genogram has been easily adapted to my own increasing interest in narrative therapy during the last several years. As trainees describe their genograms, I also ask them to relate mythic stories about gender from their family. These stories form the basis for an analysis of the gender beliefs and roles in the trainee's family, and can be contrasted with the corresponding beliefs of the client's family.

Another technique that I have used over the years is the reversal, in which I ask the trainee to repeat the clinical dilemma reversing the genders of the clients, as a check on how gendered the dilemma is. This is also a good way to test balance and fairness in the relationship: would the same request, concern, or demand sound equally reasonable if it were said in the voice of the other gender? Like most supervisors, I frequently assign readings to my trainees: books and articles by feminists such as Carol Gilligan, Virginia Goldner, Harriet Lerner, the women at the Stone Center and those of The Women's Project in Family Therapy.

When all is said and done, the most important thing I probably do as a feminist supervisor is to provide a context in which gender is always regarded as an integral, legitimate topic of concern in therapy. My own continuing struggle with questions of gender mirrors and validates the struggles of my trainees. Since supervision is isomorphic to therapy, I try to establish relationships with my trainees that are respectful, honest, collaborative, and empowering. I draw connections between our work and our lives, pointing out, for example, how difficult it can be to do marital therapy when your own primary relationship is in the midst of a fight. I try to be fully present in supervision, sharing my own countertransference reactions to their clients, as well as my own occasional despair over my inability to help every client.

One of the areas where my vision of supervision as a collaborative relationship is most clear to me is in the conduct of live supervision sessions. When I was a trainee, one of the most disempowering, even humiliating experiences I had was having a supervisor come into sessions I was conducting and take them over. Both the clients and I would be left with the feeling that I didn't know what I was doing. Over the years, I have noticed that most of my male colleagues cannot resist this urge.

I have two rules about intruding into a trainee's session during a live interview. First, I resist the urge to go in as long as possible. Since I have been doing therapy for more than twenty years, it is axiomatic that I could do the session better than the trainee. My goal is to help the trainee have the very best session she or he could have. Calling in with suggestions or calling the trainee out of the session are far less disruptive to the process than my going in. Second, if I do feel the need to be part of the session, I stay for as brief a time as possible and I am very careful to hand the session back to the trainee before I leave.

Recently, I told the trainees in my supervision group that I am going to take a leave of absence next year from my academic and administrative responsibilities at FI in order to slow my life down, pursue some training for myself, and generally reduce stress in my life. I had dreaded making this announcement, expecting that they would be angry or feel abandoned. Instead, I received enthusiastic support for my decision. In our ensuing discussion, the members of my supervision group let me know that they considered my decision congruent with the values they were being taught in the training program and, further, that my decision reaffirmed each of their desires to live a coherent, balanced life.

THE CLASSROOM CONTEXT

As long as the relationships between me and my trainees are contained in supervision, they are an unambiguous pleasure. However, in the larger contexts of the training program, such as the classroom, the alliances are more complicated. At FI the classroom teaching is done by the senior staff, who take turns lecturing on various topics. Supervisors as well as trainees often attend the lectures. In the first couple of years that I was at FI, my trainees were almost the only ones to ask questions about gender in class. Their questions were sometimes annoying to the lecturer; in the beginning, they were certainly unexpected. On those occasions when I was in the classroom as such questions were asked, I found myself needing to advocate for the trainee's right to a serious response while avoiding becoming triangled between the trainee and my colleague. This was even harder to do when I was *not* in the classroom, but would have the exchange recounted to me later in supervision. I learned the importance of not taking on the issue as my own, but rather helping the trainee develop a strategy for getting a satisfactory answer to his or her question.

BRINGING GENDER TO THE CURRICULUM

When I arrived at FI in 1989, there was no mention of gender in the curriculum. The simplest first order change I suggested was the addition of several lectures on the topics of the feminist critique of family therapy, bringing gender into the therapy room, men's issues, and gender inequities in marriage and marital therapy. There was no resistance from the rest of the faculty. A young male colleague (i.e., with low status) took the men's issues lecture; I did the other three. This was the simplest, least painful, and certainly the least systemic solution to the problem. I could lecture freely on these topics, the trainees were always enthused, and the rest of the faculty weren't perturbed. Eventually, the *trainees* became perturbed, as they grasped how separate from the main body of the theory and method they were learning the issue of gender stood.

In my third year at FI, we undertook to achieve greater integration of the issues of gender and culture into the curriculum. This was a bold and complex step, which is not yet close to being fully achieved. We opened up the entire curriculum to evaluation about how adequately it included concepts of gender and culture. Four years later, this process is not complete. The further we get into it, the more complex the process becomes.

We began by looking at how our case examples and videotapes reflected the gender and cultural composition of our trainees and their cases. We looked for subtle biases in the conceptual material in the lectures. This process was challenging, in that it required accepting that gender and culture were critical variables and simultaneously acknowledging that we were often biased in our consideration (or, more typically, our lack of consideration) of these variables.

COLLEGIAL RELATIONSHIPS

When you start looking at how gender affects your clinical work and teaching, it is but a very small step to looking at how it affects your collegial relationships. For me, this is the heart of the matter. The motto "the personal is the political" is as true in the office as in the bedroom. The isomorphism between how gender is construed in the relationships between faculty colleagues and how it is presented in the training program is unavoidable. This is the most aggravating, challenging aspect of being part of an institute that is not feminist in its mission. When I was a feminist among feminists (i.e., at WILS), I could make assumptions about our shared beliefs and practices. If any of us got temporarily woolly-headed about gender, we could count on someone else to call attention to it. At FI, I have no such safety net. Particularly in my early years at FI, if I did not comment on gender, it was more than likely that no one else would either. At times, feeling gender as a unique responsibility of mine has been a burden. I have had the experience of waking in the middle of the night with anxiety about some sexist statement or action that happened at work the day before which I did not have the wits to challenge at the time.

On the other hand, living among the heathen, as it were, has its uses. Since I can't count on the instant understanding of all my colleagues when I want to bring up an issue about gender, I think I have learned to become more articulate, and to reason more closely. I have also internalized the belief that you can't win 'em all (at least I can't); some arguments I have learned to leave for another day.

One important difference between FI and WILS has to do with the level of trust between colleagues. WILS was small, intimate, feminine and feminist. FI is large, sometimes impersonal, and not feminist. Taking risks at FI seems, well, *riskier.* It is harder to get beneath the surface to confront the gender issues between us as men and women. Challenging someone who is personally, as well as professionally, committed to you is very different than challenging a colleague with whom you have little personal relationship and much lower trust. Some of my conversations with male colleagues about this issue bear painful similarity to the conversations I witness again and again in marital therapy: she says: "This isn't fair" and he says "I can't deal with your anger." But then, why would our conversations be different? Why shouldn't we expect ourselves to trip over the same habits of behavior and uses of power that our clients trip over? This is both the bane and the hope of life in a nonfeminist institute for me. It is a laboratory in which all the gendered dynamics of male-female relationships occur with maddening and predictable regularity. And, for that very reason, it also holds the possibility of being an environment in which these dynamics can be challenged, overcome, and reformulated.

IF I KNEW THEN . . .

Two decades and three institutes into my life as a feminist family therapist, what I have learned about training in this context comes down to this:

1. For the feminist trainer, it is essential to have regular access to other feminists. Being in conversation with others who share similar views reduces the pain of living in intellectual isolation and also stimulates and supports the development of more refined thinking about feminist questions.
2. Confronting patriarchy and sexism is a project that requires endurance. The issues are as likely to emerge around subtle distinctions of language and small bits of behavior as around diagnostic labeling or misogynist interventions, perhaps even more so. Changing the hearts and minds of colleagues and trainees is a long-term, multifaceted project. In my experience, it has been most successful when I have already established a trusting and respectful relationship with the other person.
3. Choose your battles well. Do not attempt to take on every gendered issue that trainees might want to hand to you. At times, encouragement and support for *their* efforts to confront issues may produce the greatest learning.
4. Never underestimate your value as a role model for the next generation. Feminist relationships are at least as powerful as feminist techniques.

REFERENCES

Goodrich, T.J., Rampage, C., Ellman, B., & Halstead, K. (1988). *Feminist family therapy: A casebook*. New York: Norton.
Hare-Mustin, R. (1978). A feminist approach to family therapy. *Family Process*, 17, 181-194.

Teaching a Feminist Family Therapy

N. Norma Akamatsu
Kathryn Basham
Mary Olson

SUMMARY. This article presents an overview of pedagogical principles based on feminist and social constructionist ideas, in the particular context of a master's degree program in social work. General approaches to the feminist enterprise of elevating subjugated voices and social constructionist emphasis on multiple perspectives are discussed, along with some specific classroom applications, and then linked to teaching about other forms of oppression. *[Article copies available from The Haworth Document Delivery Service: 1-800-342-9678. E-mail address: getinfo@haworth.com]*

This article emerges from conversations among five women who teach family systems theory and/or practice at the Smith College School for Social Work, three of whom collaborated to write this paper. Individual differences have been muted in favor of the con-

N. Norma Akamatsu, MSW, Kathryn Basham, PhD, and Mary Olson, MSW, are faculty at the Smith School for Social Work.

Address correspondence to N. Norma Akamatsu at the Northampton Institute for Family Therapy, 151 Main Street, Northampton, MA 01060.

The authors express grateful appreciation to Dean Emeritus Ann Hartman, DSW, for her unfailing support of their exploration and growth as teachers; also to their co-conversationalists, Phebe Sessions, PhD, and Joan Laird, MSW, who was especially generous in sharing her ideas; and, finally, to Michele Bograd and Kathy Weingarten for their extensive editorial help.

gruence in teaching principles that we discovered was predominant. Similarly, our different relationships to the institutional context, based on years at Smith or adjunct versus full-time position, have not been detailed. A brief description of the institutional context follows as background to the discussion of feminist pedagogy which forms the central part of our discussion.

Smith College, founded in 1871, was among the earliest institutions in this country dedicated to the education of young women, one of the "Seven Sisters" to the formerly all-male "Ivy League" and remains today among the few undergraduate institutions for women only. The School for Social Work was founded in 1917 in response to the need for mental health professionals to work with psychologically disabled veterans returning from World War I. Since that time, psychodynamic perspectives have defined the School's intellectual and institutional identity.

In the context of this history, the installation of Ann Hartman, a Dean strongly identified with family therapy, was a source of some anxiety and disturbance for some a decade ago. Only one participant in the conversations leading to this article taught prior to the arrival of the now-retired Dean Hartman whose tenure was characterized by a process of increasing acceptance of family therapy, incorporation of a feminist critique, and greater attention to the changing social context.

Today the School for Social Work is coeducational but, as within the field generally, men are a distinct minority. The average age of the very bright, idealistic, and often challenging body of students, hovers around 30. The intellectual culture of the School is now strongly feminist and includes an increasingly visible lesbian feminist presence, particularly among students, but also of administrators and faculty, who find support and affirmation in the surrounding community, a (comparatively) accepting environment. Under the leadership of Dean Hartman, the School also made special efforts to recruit students of color, whose voices are becoming more prominent in the evolving culture of the School.

The curricula and teachers are routinely evaluated by students and questioned specifically about attention paid to issues of gender, including sexual orientation, racism, and ethnic difference. Student feedback indicates that typically in family therapy courses, feminist perspectives have been well integrated. We attribute this to the vigor of the feminist critique in our field which includes the articulation of principles applicable to the process of education. What follows is a summary of approaches that are probably characteristic of much feminist family therapy training that were identified in our conversations about our own teaching.

PRINCIPLES FOR INTEGRATING A FEMINIST PERSPECTIVE

Foucault (1980) has described feminism as the insurrection of subjugated knowledge. In our view, bringing a feminist stance to the teaching of family therapy theory and practice means to create space for previously marginalized voices to be heard. Some general principles, shared among the authors, form the underpinnings of our efforts to support and extend the "insurrection."

Social Constructionism and Multiple Perspectives: Social constructionist theory provides the epistemological "holding environment" which allows us both to notice and receive diverse perspectives (Gergen, 1991; Hoffman, 1990; Laird, 1995; MacNamee & Gergen, 1992). Rejecting the notion of objective reality in favor of a view of socially negotiated interpretations encourages us to attend to many voices: "With the advent of social constructionism, the 'universe' of modernism gives way to a 'multiverse' " (Pare, 1995, p. 11). This is an invitation to entertain diversity in all its manifestations, including a recognition of multiple feminisms as well as other forms of oppression. Social constructionism, including a critique of its own assumptions or limitations, is central to our feminist family therapy teaching.

Deconstruction: A feminist stance, in large measure, *is* a deconstructionist stance which White (1993) relates to

> procedures that subvert taken-for-granted realities and practices; those so-called "truths" that are split off from the conditions and the context of their production, those disembodied ways of speaking that hide their biases and prejudices, and those familiar practices of self and of relationship that are subjugating of persons' lives. (p. 34)

This activity makes more apparent the processes by which women's knowledges, and the gendered knowledges of men, have been subjugated. Our attention is directed at the shaping contexts—social, economic, and political—which result in this and other effects. Deconstruction is the analytic inquiry that grounds our social constructionist orientation in the larger contexts that have always been a part of social work.

Infusion of Feminist Content: We begin with an assumption that challenges the idea of woman as "other" or a pedagogy of "add women and stir." Instead, we propose that a feminist or gendered lens must be threaded throughout the curriculum, integrated into every course, every unit, and even into every class.

Re-Authoring History and Heroines: Students must be helped to claim their role models, both historically and in the present. The problem of invisibility has characterized the history of all oppressed groups. The stories of the great women of social work are at times suppressed, for example in our school, in favor of the great men who developed psychoanalytic thought. In family therapy courses, a condensed history may reflect only the contributions of a few white, heterosexual men defined as founders of "schools," obscuring the contributions of the women with whom they worked. Women need to gain control over their own storying in the present and their own history-making. Teachers, then, need to interrogate the historical canon, reclaiming lost contributions and energetically crediting new ones.

Decentering: Several ideas from feminist thought flow into this principle of "pivoting the center." We attempt to shift our focus, at times moving "from margin to center" (hooks, 1984). The teacher may *begin* from the perspective of the marginalized, foregoing loyalty to the socially sanctioned world view and, especially, to the dominant canon. So, for example, we have often used a selection from feminist theory as the introductory reading for our family theory survey course (such as Gordon's, 1988, " 'Be Careful About Father': Incest, Girls' Resistance, and the Construction of Femininity," *Heroes of Their Own Lives: The Politics and History of Family Violence*, or Goldner's, 1985, groundbreaking article, "Feminism and Family Therapy"). Similarly, we can start with the experiences of women in families of color or lesbian families, then move to the single mother or single father family and finally to the family headed by a heterosexual couple. "Normative" definitions of family are not limited to any category.

Strengths Perspective: A fundamental aspect of the "feminist insurrection" has been the recognition of psychological double standards that tend to devalue or pathologize women for enacting the very gender roles they are socialized into. An insistent skepticism about theories that define standards of "health" and questioning who exactly is doing the defining are an integral aspect of a deconstructive feminist analysis. Consequently, we approach our teaching with an emphasis on strengths, rather than a "deficit" perspective, in conjunction with some critical inquiry about how the definition of "deficit" was arrived at. This analysis highlights the unequal power relationship between practitioner and client (or, by implication, between teacher and student) in terms of who gets to define whom and the many pragmatic implications of that power.

Translating these principles into classroom activity adds another dimension to the discussion of a feminist approach to teaching that begins with the student-teacher relationship.

FEMINIST PEDAGOGY

The central critique offered in Freire's *Pedagogy of the Oppressed* (1971), centers on his shift from the "banking model" of education in which the teacher/expert "deposits" knowledge into the empty account of the student/non-expert. Freire proposes instead a "midwife model" in which learning is a two-way process. His feminine image of the midwife and dedication to freeing the colonized *mind* make his work particularly suited to feminist goals in education. According to Freire, teaching is not about imparting truth, per se, but creating the capacity to be in dialogue with cultural traditions, thus fostering the development of a critical consciousness. Instead of learning to adopt positions, students learn to form their own thoughts. For women, this process counteracts the invalidation of female students that occurs within many male-dominated institutions. We are not equating feminism in education simply with a difference in process, since there are the missing texts of women's history and achievements that also need to be recognized. However, without fostering the students' capacities to speak their own voices, the feminist teacher could be supplanting patriarchal truths with feminist truths without facilitating the student's sense of agency and empowered capacity to evaluate knowledge (including feminist claims) and generate meaning.

The research of Belenky et al. (1986) applies the insights of Freire to women's education. This study shows how the construction of voice emerges from the process of collaboration. Another important distinction relates to their notion of voice, which goes beyond "point of view" and connotes a whole psychological, social, and moral configuration. The conception of self is interpersonal, based on Gilligan's (1982) realm of the "different voice" in which the web of connection replaces hierarchy, and relationships—not abstract principles—are primary.

As female teachers with mostly female students, we have found such ideas to be of utmost value with all our students. We have translated them into specific principles within our teaching: confirmation, collaborative dialogue, transparency and reflexivity (the reflecting process). We believe that such principles are interwoven with a teaching process that respects the authority, knowledge, and voice of the teacher as well.

As noted by Belenky's group, many women enter educational institutions with doubt and uncertainty about their abilities. They benefit from acknowledgement at the beginning of their education, especially a sense of community and confirmation, in contrast to the male model of "commencement" in which the endpoint, graduation, represents acceptance by the elders into the scholarly tribe. In our experience, this prerequisite of acceptance is critical for students. They are met with interest and curiosity about their thinking, rather than doubt and criticism. We assume a stance of affirmation in which an understanding of the person is central, rather than impersonal standards. We attempt to constitute an "honoring community" (Lynn Hoffman, personal communication, 1995) which emphasizes recognition rather than evaluation.

Opening rituals are a common practice in our courses to bring the class together as a group and communicate the value placed on the experiential and interactive in our learning. We use the time-honored exercise of telling the history of a person's name (Roberts,

1988), relating what "family" means to the individual student, or identifying the aspects of family theory that are compatible with one's preferred values (White, 1992b).

Collaborative dialogue is also a key interaction in feminist-oriented teaching. Teachers and students think out loud, together, involved in a process of critical reflection. Such an orientation does not preclude lecturing or the presentation of material, but we find it useful to interweave our own expertise with dialogue with students. The principle of transparency (White, 1993) is also important here—the deconstructive effort to situate our own knowledge and perspectives within the contexts, both personal and intellectual, in which they arose, to bring our "truths" back to "the conditions and the context of their production." In this way we share our own relationship to ideas, rather than presenting them as objects.

The reflecting process (Andersen, 1987) is a format we frequently use that can be adapted to many situations–case presentations, role plays, or as a closing exercise for a course. The reflecting process shapes the class differently by defining discussion as meaning-making and knowledge as emergent. It elicits the knowledge of the student, rather than making the teacher's knowledge the sole focus of learning, and promotes the open examination, or deconstruction, of both the teacher's and students' contributions. Students typically remark on the experience of the reflecting team as very positive.

Our courses combine feminist epistemology with postmodern formats that emphasize the construction of voice through interpersonal communication. We interweave the teaching of new knowledge and skills with encouraging students to trust their own ideas and perceptions. The principles of confirmation, collaboration, transparency, and reflexivity are consistent with the goals of an emancipatory education and allow us not only to teach a feminist perspective but· to enact one by recognizing and supporting the capacities of our students.

THE CLASSROOM MILIEU

Establishing an interactive "holding environment" of trust and the open discussion of conflicting views is a key ingredient in promoting active discourse involving multiple perspectives. Clarification of goals helps set the stage. In the first class it is often illuminating for students to hear that, along with the usual list of particular learning objectives, the course purpose includes creation of a complex learning environment in which differing ideas and opinions are encouraged. Group norms, defined as expectations for collegial interaction, should also be reviewed at the outset. These might include assumptions that students will listen to each other with curiosity, foster their capacity for empathy for others' positions, and engage in respectful dialogue. At times, it is helpful to refer to some foundation communication skills regarding active listening, use of "I" positions (that reflect the individual student's actual ideas, opinions, or feelings) in lieu of "you" positions (that cast blame or overgeneralize about other people). This emphasis at the beginning supports the development of a learning frame that reduces anxiety about dealing with conflict.

It is the instructor's responsibility to be clear and firm about the parameters of constructive dialogue. There are unfortunate examples of classes that have derailed under the guise of collaborative teaching, when an instructor has failed to protect students from a destructive exchange. For example, in a class on multiculturalism and clinical practice, a student who struggled with her own internalized bigotry toward Latino persons, expressed some negative and painful stereotypes. Another student quickly interrupted with a harsh epithet: "How could you be such a bigot? You are truly ignorant!" Such stereotypes, attacks, and name-calling must be interrupted by the instructor. Even when students respond to violations of group norms, the instructor should assume responsibility, not only for promoting constructive interactions, but also to interrupt destructive talk.

In all discussions of diversity in the classroom, students are encouraged to be alert to any sign of biases on the part of self or other, including the instructor. Hare-Mustin's concept of alpha and beta bias (1989) is very useful. The realization of occasional bias and error among both students and faculty is crucial in role modeling a valuation of diversity without expecting the unrealistic burden of constant political correctness. This requires that the instructor truly be open to feedback, with a commitment to reduce personal defensiveness in the face of negative feedback.

An example of alpha bias emerged in a particular class in Family Theory. After disseminating a favorite cartoon to the class of twenty-three students, an instructor anticipated the usual response of delighted amusement. However, a raised hand signaled a rebuke that "It looked as if *you*, like other teachers, had chosen once again to stereotype men negatively." The cartoon features a young prehistoric man enthusiastically pointing to his genogram while the female teacher and classmates look on. Ancestors are depicted as Cro-Magnon men and women along with earlier descendants that appear to be amoebas. In any event, the student felt that the instructor had slipped into alpha bias. According to his perspective, a cartoon that negatively and stereotypically presented males as "ignorant cavemen" had purposefully been chosen. With just a twinge of defensiveness, the instructor asked if he noticed that the depictions of the cave women ancestors were not especially flattering either. He agreed, but pursued the complaint with a generalizing comment that men are depicted in a very negative light in many courses in the program since "it has such a strong feminist orientation." Following an initial defensiveness, the instructor then gratefully practiced what she had been recommending to students. "Let's stop for a moment . . . and try to empathize with this position." She reflected that this example among many others might reinforce the notion of generalizing and stereotyping if there were not a continuous effort to call forth the balance. The male student and others proceeded to talk about the capacity of many men to be both empathic and sensitive, attributes that challenge the "caveman" stereotype.

In a different class on Couple Therapy, the notion of beta bias was challenged. A student presented a case of a lesbian couple who requested therapy. The student mentioned that she thought the most important issues were concerns regarding intimacy, distribution of power, and communication skills, themes that are universal for all couples. Another student angrily blurted out: "How could you be so insensitive!" The instructor interrupted the discussion and asked the class to look at what had just occurred. After one student voiced the group norm to express feelings and ideas directly and avoid judgmental remarks, the distressed student proceeded to relate how angry and hurt she had felt that the issues of societal and internalized homophobia were not considered at all in the case presentation. She explained clearly how painful this is for homosexual clients as compared with heterosexual couples, thus contextualizing how the beta bias had developed in this instance.

Establishing a collaborative classroom "holding environment" directly implements feminist and social constructionist principles and is facilitated by attention to group process and active discussion of the inevitable interplay of alpha and beta biases.

A FEMINISM COGNIZANT OF OTHER OPPRESSIONS

A strong feminist perspective can run the risk of creating a tunnel vision that excludes perspectives on other oppressive contexts. As social work educators, preparing students to confront the full array of social issues, we are committed to teaching a feminist family therapy that remains alert to other forms of oppression, such as racism, heterosexism, able-bodism, classism, and ageism.

Women of color have consistently pointed to the inevitable impact of racism in their assessment of the meaning of gender inequality in their lives, noting the failure of white feminists to distinguish the differential effects of a white patriarchy on the lives of people of color. Two African-American feminists, over a 14-year timespan, emphasize the same points. In 1980, the poet and social critic, Audre Lorde, pointed out: "There is a pretense of homogeneity of experience covered by the word sisterhood that does not in fact exist" (1984, p. 116). More recently, the psychologist, Beverly Greene (1994), reiterates:

A consistent and problematic theme throughout feminist therapy literature and a barrier to diversity within feminist therapy theory is the assumption that gender is the primary locus of oppression for all women. . . . A subtle but salient consequence of this assumption is that it overlooks the privileged status of being white, regardless of gender oppression . . .

Formidable obstacles sustain this overlooking. First is the invisibility of privilege, observed so acutely by McIntosh (1989), that remains hidden within the pervasive cultural sanctioning of white supremacy as "normal." Secondly, as McGoldrick (1994) points out, we see ourselves more easily as "objects" of injury than as "subjects" having the power to cause harm. The confrontation with one's own racial, heterosexual, and/or socioeconomic privilege, recognition of the benefits automatically conferred and, more pointedly, that we accept and utilize, can be a very painful and identity-shifting awakening, aptly termed a "disintegration" experience (Helms, 1990).

While this level of confrontation with privilege may be outside the scope of the ordinary family therapy course, some consideration is critical and implicit in the feminist teaching we have been discussing. The social constructionist perspective on the self provides a starting place. When the self is revisioned as a "communal creation" (Gergen, 1991, p. 140), realized in interaction, the concept of identity is transfigured: "[T]he idea of many selves for many contexts becomes an alternative way of knowing" (Penn & Frankfurt, 1994, p. 222). Totalizing and either/or definitions of self can give way to a more nuanced and context-sensitive "multiplexity."[1] More specifically, the paradoxical experience that we may be disadvantaged in some contexts, yet privileged in others, becomes more apparent. Andrea Ayvazian, a white anti-bias activist, emphasizes this:

> We . . . know that everyone has multiple social identities—we are all dominant and targeted simultaneously. I am, in the very same moment, dominant as a white person and targeted as a woman. A white able-bodied man may be dominant in those categories, but targeted as a Jew or as a gay person. (1995, p. 17)

Reinforcing such "multiplexity" in the classroom can be encouraged in many ways. Waldegrave (1990) discusses the use of "cultural consultants" in the "Just Therapy" developed at The Family Center of New Zealand. Members of indigenous cultures provide feedback about the relevance of therapeutic work to their particular ethnic/racial group. What is notable in this practice is that the therapy is held accountable to these cultural consultants. Students or faculty can serve in a similar capacity and offer their personal experience within a given social context (socioeconomic, ethnic, racial, or gendered) as a way to expand others' sensitivity to an unfamiliar territory. However, it is vitally important that this is a totally voluntary and strongly supported activity since, as many have pointed out (e.g., Lorde, 1984), the burden of teaching is habitually placed on the oppressed. "I am tired of being The Experience for white students," an African-American woman protested. This also runs the risk of exacerbating the lack of responsibility taken by those in power to initiate the examination of the inequities in which they participate.

Segments from popular movies can also support a "decentered" perspective that provides diverse images of families. Recently, for example, we have used scenes from *The Joyluck Club, The Wedding Banquet, Boyz N the Hood, Hoop Dreams* and *The Great Santini* to talk about the experience of Asian-American mothers and daughters, gay couples, poor African-American families, and family violence in a white, middle-class family.

Alternatively, the development of a particular kind of reflexivity, an attempt to stand outside of and observe one's own position of privilege, can be fostered. Members from dominant groups can be designated as "emissaries" who choose to listen through the lenses of marginalized groups for the relevance of theory and appropriateness of practice to their needs. While clearly limited, this attempt at "empathic impersonation" (Penn & Frankfurt, 1994) may allow students to move beyond their usual perspective and struggle to discern another's experience. We have found such a revisioning invaluable, for example, in discussions of "family life cycle" frameworks which so often institutionalize the defunct "Ozzie & Harriet" ideal. The experiences of gay and lesbian family members, people of color, non-European ethnic groups, single parents, and childless couples have all been made more salient by using this device in the classroom. A similar reexamination is potentiated in the way Hoffman (personal communication, 1994) conducts what she calls "share-vision"–as distinguished from "supervision." She interviews the clinician and uses the structure of a reflecting team to provide commentary and amplify on this exchange. She also specifically requests that some team members "stand in" for the family (see also, White, 1995). In this way their imagined perspective and response to the entire conversation become a living part of the procedure and team members are, again, called upon to grapple with the particularities experienced by people of possibly quite different backgrounds. Another especially important aspect of reflexivity is considering how members of dominant groups may, themselves, be perceived: imagining others imagining you. This "empathic impersonation" often makes the invisible mantle of privilege more apparent. Some useful questions include: how might clients of color perceive white male or white female therapists or experience a predominantly white agency; how might therapists of color feel in these same contexts? The question of stereotyping was addressed by asking what stereotypes clients of color might anticipate encountering and by considering what stereotypes white therapists anticipate encountering and rehearsing ways to respond to these unspoken negative expectations.

Deconstructive inquiry is another way to highlight the impact of social contexts and help students develop "thicker" descriptions that emphasize the intersection of gender issues with those of race, class, culture, and sexual orientation. Explorations which bring gender role choices into awareness and conversation (Sheinberg & Penn, 1991; White, 1992a) can be extended to include these other perspectives. For example, cross-cultural and cross-generational differences can be confronted and contextualized (Akamatsu, 1995). Helpful questions include:

What is the traditional role of women in your culture, as you understand that based on your particular family experience? What aspects of the traditional role did women in your family follow and what aspects did they not follow? What are the stories about such women? What experiences committed them to these positions?

How did living in the United States impact on the traditional role? How was it for male family members when women did not follow the traditional role?

In what ways do you see yourself following a traditional role; in what ways not? Do you see yourself as similar to or different from your mother/daughter in this regard?

Since different social contexts call up different aspects of our multiple identities, areas of vulnerability or privilege, questions which deconstruct these multiplexities help guard against a reductionistic approach that can lead to misunderstandings–or a simplistic "us versus them" conceptualization.

The feminist viewpoint advanced throughout this discussion invites collaboration and the participation of multiple voices, especially those that have been marginalized or subjugated. The ethical concern with encouraging the development of voice, the self-in-relation (Gilligan, 1982; Olson, 1994), directs our attention to other experiences of oppression. As political and economic forces increasingly threaten to divide and conquer some of us more than others, these connections become more vital and more tenuous. Our sense of oppression is a double-edged sword. The need for validation of the pain of the particular injustice we have experienced can drive us into a symmetrical, isolating competition to be heard. At the same time, acknowledgement of our common, although different and unique, experiences of marginalization can form a connecting arc/ark of mutual recognition that may advance our cause(s) from a broader foundation and with greater power.

CONCLUSION

As social workers, we share a unique collective identity as a profession committed to a practice that embraces a value system, in which women predominate. Historically, ours is also a field through which the working class and women have attained professional status, a legacy of empowerment. Social workers have also played a unique and important role in the field of family therapy, often in the direction of an expanded view of social context.

In this article, we have outlined an orientation to teaching that seems to us consistent with a feminist agenda, broadly defined as the "insurrection of subjugated voices." While recognizing the existence of numerous feminisms and the varying emphases designated by terms like cultural or political feminism, we have concentrated on general principles that rely on the social constructionist perspective that we believe is supportive of the diversity and multiplicity of voices the we actively seek to engage. In this endeavor, we have rediscovered the futility of dichotomizing the cognitive and affective, thinking and feeling, theory and interpersonal milieu. The principles identified–social constructionism, deconstruction, decentering, collaboration, dialogic process, and affirmation–repeatedly link personal experience with the group process and the social context. In the ten years since the gathering storm of feminist criticism rained in force upon the field of family therapy, changes in our practice, theory, and professional organizations have ensued. The articulation and elaboration of a feminist pedagogy represents another important benchmark. Although the insurrection is far from concluded, perhaps this is a time to take stock and consider future directions. Now that we have developed some sense of what we have learned and ways of teaching consistent with this learning, where shall we take it next?

NOTE

1. A term used by Cornel West in a dialogue on Black-Jewish relations with Michael Lerner, October, 1995, Mt. Holyoke College, South Hadley, MA.

REFERENCES

Akamatsu, N. (1995). The defiant daughter and compliant mother: Multicultural dialogues on woman's role. *In Session: Psychotherapy in Practice*, 1, 43-55.

Andersen, T. (1987). The reflecting team: Dialogue and metadialogue in clinical work. *Family Process*, 26, 425-428.

Ayvazian, A. (1995). Interrupting the cycle of oppression: The role of allies as agents of change. *Smith College School for Social Work Journal*, 13, 17-20.

Belenky, M., Clinchy, B., Goldberger, N. & Tarule, J. (1986). *Women's Ways of Knowing*. New York: Basic Books.

Foucault, M. (1980). *Power/Knowledge: Selected Interviews and Other Writings*. New York: Pantheon Press.

Freire, P. (1971). *Pedagogy of the Oppressed*. New York: Seaview.

Gergen, K. (1991). *The Saturated Self: Dilemmas of Identity in Contemporary Life*. New York: Basic Books.

Gilligan, C. (1982). *In a Different Voice: Psychological Theory and Women's Development*. Cambridge: Harvard University Press.

Goldner, V. (1985). Feminism and family therapy. *Family Process*, 24, 31-47.

Gordon, L. (1988). "Be careful about father": Incest, girls' resistance, and the construction of femininity. In *Heroes of Their Own Lives: The Politics and History of Family Violence*. New York: Viking.

Greene, B. (1994). Diversity and difference: Race and feminist psychotherapy. In M. Mirkin, *Women in Context: Toward A Feminist Reconstruction of Psychotherapy*. New York: Guilford Press.

Hare-Mustin, R. (1989). The problem of gender in family therapy theory. In M. McGoldrick, C. Anderson & F. Walsh (Eds.), *Women in Families: A Framework for Family Therapy.* New York: W.W. Norton.

Helms, J. (Ed.) (1990). *Black and White Racial Identity: Theory, Research and Practice.* Westport, CT: Greenwood Press.

Hoffman, L. (1990). Constructing realities: An art of lenses. *Family Process,* 29, 1-12.

Hoffman, L. (1994). Personal communication.

Hoffman, L. (1995). Personal communication.

hooks, b. (1984). *Feminist Theory from Margin to Center.* New York: Crossing Press.

Laird, J. (1995). Family-centered practice: Feminism, constructionism and cultural perspectives. In N. van den Bergh, *Feminist Practice in the 21st Century,* 20-40. Washington, DC: NASW Press.

Lorde, A. (1984). Age, race, class and sex: Women redefining difference. In *Sister Outsider.* Trumansberg, NY: The Crossing Press.

MacNamee, S. & Gergen, K. (Eds.) (1992). *Therapy as Social Construction.* London: Sage Publications.

McGoldrick, M. (1994). The ache for home. *Family Therapy Networker,* 18, 38-45.

McIntosh, P. (1989, July/August). White privilege: Unpacking the invisible knapsack. *Peace and Freedom,* 10-12.

Olson, M. (1994). Conversation and writing: A collaborative approach to bulimia. *Journal of Feminist Family Therapy,* 6, 21-44.

Pare, D. (1995). Of families and other cultures: The shifting paradigm of family therapy. *Family Process,* 34, 1-19.

Penn, P. & Frankfurt, M. (1994). Creating a participant text: Writing, multiple voices, narrative multiplicity. *Family Process,* 33, 217-231.

Roberts, J. (1988). *Rituals and Family Therapy.* New York: W.W. Norton.

Sheinberg, M. & Penn, P. (1991). Gender dilemmas, gender questions and the gender mantra. *Journal of Marital and Family Therapy,* 17, 33-44.

Waldegrave, C. (1990). Social justice in family therapy. *Dulwich Centre Newsletter,* 1.

White, M. (1992a). Men's culture, men's movement, and the constitution of men's lives. *Dulwich Centre Newsletter,* 3 & 4, 33-52.

White, M. (1992b). Presentation at the Ackerman Institute for Family Therapy, October 1992.

White, M. (1993). Deconstruction and therapy. In S. Gilligan & R. Price (Eds.), *Therapeutic Conversations.* New York: W.W. Norton.

White, M. (1995). Reflecting teamwork as definitional ceremony. In *Re-Authoring Lives: Interviews and Essays.* Adelaide, So. Australia: Dulwich Centre Publications.

Finding Ways to Attend to and Talk About Family Therapy and Feminism from "Non-Mainstream" Paths

Pilar Hernandez

SUMMARY. In this paper I revisit my training experience in the family therapy specialty at a counseling program. The basic question I am addressing is how meaning is constructed out of social experiences and memory. Taking a feminist and family therapy orientations as a starting point, I consider the interaction between personal narratives and clinical theories, and the implication of this interaction for therapy. In particular, I examine my experience with silence as a mark of social constraint but also as a sign of struggle. I suggest that certain narrative approaches involving collaborative negotiations of meaning can productively address the issue of silence. Finally, I suggest that "narrativizing" can provide a mapping function to the maze of discontinuities that arise in social interaction, especially in the case of cultural dislocations. *[Article copies available from The Haworth Document Delivery Service: 1-800-342-9678. E-mail address: getinfo@haworth.com]*

Pilar Hernandez is a doctoral candidate in the Family Therapy specialty of the School and Counseling Psychology Program, University of Massachusetts.

Address correspondence to the author at Hills South, School of Education, School and Counseling Psychology, University of Massachusetts, Amherst, MA 01003.

The author expresses her great appreciation to Kathy Weingarten and Michele Bograd for their comments and support in the writing of this paper, and to Janine Roberts for her guidance and words of wisdom.

[Haworth co-indexing entry note]: "Finding Ways to Attend to and Talk About Family Therapy and Feminism from 'Non-Mainstream' Paths." Hernandez, Pilar. Co-published simultaneously in *Journal of Feminist Family Therapy* (The Haworth Press, Inc.) Vol. 8, No. 2, 1996, pp. 37-52; and: *Reflections on Feminist Family Therapy Training* (ed: Kathy Weingarten, and Michele Bograd) The Haworth Press, Inc., 1996, pp. 37-52. Single or multiple copies of this article are available from The Haworth Document Delivery Service [1-800-342-9678, 9:00 a.m. - 5:00 p.m. (EST). E-mail address: getinfo@haworth.com].

As a Latin American woman working and studying in the field of family therapy and as a feminist concerned with integrating a feminist approach to family therapy, I was asked to write about my educational experience in family therapy training. I write this paper from the perspective of a woman raised in Latin America. I was born and raised in Colombia and I came to the USA four and a half years ago for graduate training. My first two years were times of continuous personal transitions, facing the challenges of learning to adjust to a new culture while "keeping" what I liked about mine. As an undergraduate at the University of the Andes in Bogota, I worked with my advisor on several projects related to women's issues, both teaching and fieldwork. My major field of study was psychology.

In this paper I will share some of my educational experiences and views that emerged when I revisited my educational experience as a doctoral student in the Family Therapy specialty of the School and Counseling Psychology program at the University of Massachusetts. The School and Counseling Psychology program, of which I am a member, is based on the practitioner-scientist model and it is strongly committed to understanding and working with social, cultural and economic diversity. The program offered the option of focusing in School and/or Counseling Psychology, while offering additional specializations in Multicultural Counseling and Family Counseling. I specialized in Family Counseling.

My experiences developed through a process where people from many different cultural backgrounds enriched me with their challenges, friendship, and ideas. I am writing my account of a process in which my learning extended beyond the walls of the classroom to informal gatherings. The ideas I will share provide an account of the way in which I have reconstructed my educational and professional experiences, trying to understand how my training has, and has not, adequately spoken to me as a woman coming from a nondominant culture facing the dominant culture of the USA.

First, I will narrate my experiences of particular educational practices and the impact they had on my professional role as a therapist. Second, I will talk about the reasons I think that some of the narrative approaches and feminist ideas have likenesses to Freire's work and why I believe that they can be useful to thinking about women's issues from a nondominant cultural perspective.

CONNECTING THE STORIES OF WHO WE ARE WITH OUR VIEWS OF CLINICAL THEORIES: WHAT CONSEQUENCES DO MY PRESENT INTERPRETATIONS OF THE PAST HAVE FOR ME IN THE FUTURE?

Even in a graduate program dedicated to working with issues of diversity, I did not always feel that my experience was at the "center" of the training. One of the group projects that we did early in the program marginalized a significant part of my past by using a "normative" discourse that did not fit my experience. Understanding how this happened provided an opportunity to develop ways to shift this and to insist on finding lenses to interpret that past that did not erase or distort my experience.

I was often asked about life in my native country, Colombia. Many times the questions seemed awkward and I did not know how to respond. I had to think and rethink what I was going to share with my classmates, trying to minimize the risk of contributing to a stereotype. I was aware that the way we framed conversations, whether formal or informal, produced dilemmas for me. My awareness of this process overwhelmed me with a sense of confusion. My confusion was a signal to me that my opinions were being reinterpreted, shaped by "alien norms." I constantly experienced tensions in having to relate and react to the way in which my very being was portrayed by others on the basis of their unquestioned assumptions. In many of the group projects we had in our classes, I found myself struggling to find ways of being "heard," often needing to challenge the very frame we were using to analyze the class materials.

One such encounter with stereotypical interpretations took place in a course that involved the study of several therapy models. The course required us to engage in theoretical discussions, write papers about models, and apply the analytical tools presented by these models to our personal work. It also involved a joint exploration of personal issues. One of the activities we engaged in was a Bowen group.

In this exercise, a group met weekly to utilize concepts of Murray Bowen to analyze our personal development and family relationships. My group was composed of three women: Chung from Japan,

Jane from New England, and myself from Colombia. Chung had arrived recently in the USA. Very early in the group project, we realized that the way she and I understood the task produced both confusion and challenge. A central theme of our conversations was our role as women in our families. We explored how family members dealt with structural issues of oppression and how our notions of oppression were determined by the context in which it was set. Chung and I were challenged when we realized that the Bowen theoretical map did not fit with how we understood issues of oppression and our identities as women in our respective countries. Our understanding was tied to the specific social and political circumstances of our countries as well as to our professional backgrounds as teachers and psychotherapists. The Bowen model did not seem to have categories to handle these contexts.

For instance, my peers in this group were intrigued about the oppression of women in Latin America. I would try to talk about that experience, but would consistently fail to make myself understood using the Bowen theoretical map. I realized that the framework I was supposed to use did not permit me to describe the context of my family's involvement in the political process of Colombia. From within the Bowen framework, that context was irrelevant. It was only when I stopped trying to fit my experience into the theory and began to share stories about what in Colombia is known as "The Violence," a prolonged and intense armed conflict between liberal and conservative parties in Colombia, that our conversations started to make sense. Retrieving the "old" stories that my grandparents used to tell enabled me to establish a context for what "individuation" and family ties meant for women in my family. I am focusing on the Bowen theory as an example of a more general phenomenon because it was the particular theory with which the class was assigned to work in small groups. However, I have no doubt that other family therapy models would have produced conundrums for me as well.

To illustrate in more detail the difficulty I had with Bowen theory, I will share some of my paternal grandmother's life, describing how both her personal choices and the violent social conditions of her time were determinants of radical changes in our family.

I begin in the late 1940s and 1950s as my paternal grandparents raise their family. My grandfather, who was involved in politics at that time, was persecuted for his views and suffered unemployment. When the rival political party was in power, there were no jobs for him. Economic resources became scarce and my grandmother decided to leave their hometown and to migrate on her own to the capital, Bogota, where she raised her three children working as a teacher for an elementary school. My grandfather stayed behind at Ibague, where the family had lived for generations. He continued to support the family as best as he could. By this time, he was landless. He shared stories with us about his family life and the traditions of that part of the country, as well as his admiration for my grandmother.

My grandmother made a decision that was completely radical for a woman of her position in those times: she left her community, even her husband, to look for better conditions to raise her children. Although societal prescriptions ruled that wives stayed with their husbands and were responsible for the household, my grandparents agreed to her leaving and this did not break their marital relationship. At that time, migration to the capital was not unknown, but it was unusual that she moved by herself, worked, studied, and reestablished the family, without breaking the family unit. After she moved, other extended family members and friends followed and connections persisted over time. No one in the family talked about the family unit as having "fallen apart." On the contrary, the connections continued and strengthened across the different places in which they all lived. My family stories were never constructed in a way that portrayed my grandparents as "divorcing," or my grandmother as escaping "oppression" from a traditional marriage. The family's story was that people were trying to help each other establish a life in a new geographical location. Adults helped with child rearing and my grandfather never lost contact with his family.

During this family transition, my family's political affiliation was strong. After migrating to the capital, our livelihood was assisted for several years through ties of kinship and of political membership. Since 1948, my country has gone through a continuous wave of political violence which has been intertwined with exploitative economic relationships. Over the years, this has developed into an unofficial civil war with incredible layers of complexity. In a society facing great societal upheaval, marital agreements, child rearing practices, and community life are developed within boundaries of particular structural constraints and possibilities. For example, when my grandmother chose to migrate, she could choose only between two cities and only one of them, Bogota, offered her conditions where she could live without a husband in the household and still secure an adequate education for her children.

This is the story I needed to tell to make sense of the roles women and men have played in my family. I needed to contextualize the concept of roles by adding a political and economic dimension. By doing so, it opened a space to see how my grandmother–who might have been seen as a "traditional woman"–was in fact a source of radical change in my family. She developed paths that opened the way for children in the succeeding generations to make changes in their choices of work and relationships and to go beyond the typical expectations of our society. My understanding of my role in the family was shaped by the logic of the themes that were prominent in my family, themes that were inextricably linked to the wider social context in which I grew up. My experiences of my family would have been dramatically distorted had the story of my family been analyzed solely through a lens that conceptualized the family as a nuclear unit. For example, extended family links might have been considered as "enmeshed" or barriers to individuation. Further, what I understood as strengths of the family might have been considered dysfunctions.

Thus, in our discussions, the process of making sense of our roles in our respective families moved from thinking in terms of acontextual categories of "I" positions to delineations of what "I" positions meant in our particular contexts. We put our views and stories at risk in sharing them with each other and agreed to interpret our roles in our families by understanding the local fabric of the family and social dynamics and their structural constraints. This process allowed us to understand and differentiate the theoretical concepts we were learning and the transformation we were making to them as we put them into practice in our contexts. This move from analyzing our lives from the preestablished categories of the theory, to an attempt to "co-create meaning and coordinate our actions to reflect mutual meaning-making" (Weingarten, 1991, p. 287) entailed our co-creation of our own meaning by situating ourselves in the history and categories of our cultures. We could no longer imagine doing our work without laying the groundwork for talking with each other about the particularities of our situation, speaking until we were "talking with each other in common terms."

WHAT WOULD HELP ME TO ADDRESS MY EXPERIENCE AS A WOMAN WITHIN THE SOCIAL CONDITIONS OF MY UPBRINGING?

Only by looking critically at the social, economic, and political issues that formed the context for my upbringing could I understand my development as a woman. That entailed analyzing the common context of struggle that women face in Colombia and acknowledging the privileges and pitfalls of my upbringing, and the particular social practices that made me "blind" to or aware of the many forms in which I experienced oppression. As a result, I was able to conceptualize myself as a therapist within the axis of the context in which I grew up and my present situation, the reconstruction that evolved of my thinking as a therapist, and the process by which my present situation occurred.

Therefore, in a training context, I would recommend that students and faculty examine the following questions to expand the relevance of Feminist Family Therapy training in general. First, in order for the group to foster the development of "common" themes emerging at the level of the specific contexts of particular life experiences, relevant questions include:

a. How do all the different family stories connect me with some social struggles of women in the Third World?
b. How does the way I tell the stories about myself connect me with some social issues and not with others?
c. How does a situated analysis of women's roles inform a feminist practice of family therapy?
d. What in my past could have predicted my career choices and my commitment to work in women's issues?

Second, in order to challenge the assumption that the "other culture" can be understood only through the perspective of one's own culture, students might instead locate issues of women and oppression at the level of the vocabularies and meanings which work to reinforce the dominant parameters. To develop conversations that expose relationships of dominance embedded in the language and concepts we use to talk to each other, the following questions can be explored:

a. Who I am talking to, who are the persons in the group, what background do they bring to discussions of "oppression"?
b. What is the predominant view in this particular group about women and oppression?
c. How is it different to talk about these issues within my own community and with people coming from another community?
d. What cultural discourses and self stories regarding women's roles in the family do people in the group bring to conversations?

Third, group members can ask themselves reflective questions about the contexts of their upbringing:

a. Are there larger issues of social unrest and oppression that are embedded in my family stories? For instance, I might ask myself, "How did the key stories about the ongoing Colombian unofficial civil war get passed down through generations? What themes were expressed in these stories? How do these stories speak to me today as someone in a 'helping profession'?"
b. If I were to reexamine or reauthor these stories, what alternative meanings could emerge?
c. What stories shed light on the "logics" of networking with an extended family?
d. When do I need coaching to jointly develop stories with my clients without imposing my own categories on them?

SILENCE MAY BE A SIGN OF STRUGGLE

While the experience in the Bowen group can be described as a way in which content can marginalize people's experience, process can too. I learned this through a particular experience of silence I had, which I eventually understood as evidence of my inadvertent collusion with educational practices that produced *one* way of constructing models and understanding facts. I have chosen to illustrate my experience of silence by describing an episode in a supervision meeting. Later, I will discuss the kinds of practices that may subvert the silencing of students whose life experiences deviate from the first world "norm."

In this episode, preconceived notions about low-income Latino families surfaced in the clinical supervision process. In a supervision class, I presented a case of a 24-year-old mother of three, who had migrated from Puerto Rico a year before and was referred by the Department of Social Services because she seemed to be depressed and required help in parenting skills. After presenting some initial information about her present family and circumstances, I was about to continue describing her migration experience when some of my colleagues jumped to comment: "Why does she have so many children?" "Isn't she Catholic?" "She has been a victim of abusive men and needs to work on protecting herself from them," etc. The discussion centered on planned parenthood, oppression, and contraceptive solutions for her. After an intense conversation about the case, I could see that she was being stigmatized as my colleagues judged her on the basis of preconceived notions about low-income Latino families. As her therapist, I was expected to take my colleagues' views as "correct" and to follow their suggestions.

I became silent after the recommendations were offered. But my silence alerted me to something that was seriously awry. I have asked myself a series of questions: What made me silent? When was my silence a sign of acceptance and when was it a warning sign indicating that certain kinds of statements were not welcome? When did silence become a sign of struggle? I also asked myself: What conditions made it possible for me to think about myself as a socially and politically situated agent? What kind of educational processes helped me name issues, verbalize problems, and take responsibility for the implications of my work?

Making meaning of my silence meant finding a way to talk about family therapy models using the categories of other cultural frameworks. It also meant paying attention and giving meaning to a particular experience I had in my body. A cue for becoming silent came from a place in my stomach. I felt a focal pain there. The pain made it hard for me to speak. I experienced this pain in specific situations where I felt that it would be hard to participate in discussions where the content of the conversations and the way the constructs were used made it impossible for me to find a way to enter with content of my own and to express my point of view. When the gap was too great, I lost my voice quietly, without really noticing how it faded as it disappeared.

I now know that my being silent was related to the lack of participants who were willing to question the culturally narrow concepts in family therapy and to explore the problems resulting from the well-meaning but insensitive application of the literature to people from nondominant cultures. The silencing of certain students may not be obvious to others. In one course we were required to indicate areas in which we wanted improvement. I noted my concern about needing to be more vocal during group discussions. My professor was surprised and expressed her perception that my participation was going well. However, further conversation revealed that there were ways in which I wanted to express myself but did not, without knowing exactly why.

My professor joined me in trying to make sense of my silence. We understood that I needed to develop a voice regarding these issues. My silence was not only about class participation. It also meant that somehow some of the class discussions were not addressing the academic and clinical issues that spoke to me as a woman from another culture. I was in a classroom where the discussions were framed within parameters that the other students took for granted. My silence was not simply personal but a sign that I was isolated. Since the discussions did not speak to my experiences, the classroom context made more prominent my concern about "silence." Had I been in a context where my concerns were shared by the majority of the voices in the classroom, I probably would have not questioned my own way of thinking about it.

NEGOTIATING MEANING:
A COLLABORATIVE LEARNING PROCESS

Making meaning out of my particular experience of silence had tremendous implications for my educational process. In breaking my silence it was essential that I shared my concern with other "quiet students" and my professor. Since the experiences and voices of certain students may be inadvertently silenced or marginalized even in a progressive program committed to multiculturalism, we looked for ways to open more spaces for participation and emphasized ways in which we could more effectively use previously designed guidelines and exercises.

I will describe experiences of mine that illustrate what I consider one of the most valuable aspects of this learning process: the continuous negotiation of meaning through group work. The constant exercise of negotiating meaning, placing our understanding of theories we were studying side by side with our understanding of our own life experiences, allowed us to maintain both an inclusive and a critical stance to the materials studied.

When we reviewed the literature on life cycles and transitions in families, we worked in pairs analyzing transition markers in our cultures and families. My partner in this endeavor was Bill from Massachusetts. Since key transitions in our families occurred in the context of religious practices, our conversations centered on the impact of being raised as Protestant or Catholic, and our moving away from these traditions. On this occasion we went beyond describing rites of passage to think about the social context in which these religious traditions were maintained and the kind of values with regard to gender that permeated the communities we lived in. My memories about my educational experience at an all-female Catholic high school were full of contradictions and I questioned the practices which had a tremendously constraining impact on our development as women. As we worked through our memories, we reframed the project to look at our personal histories from two perspectives: (a) our family's role within the social fabric and its particular gender politics and (b) how our current behavior could be more congruent with the values we wanted to embrace.

Another situation that required an integration or negotiation of family therapy models and our personal experience was an exercise in which we were expected to compare the family dynamics in well-known fictional and dramatic works with the dynamics of our own families. We could choose from among a long list of alternative novels and plays, or our own sources. We worked on a comprehensive paper that included: (a) an analysis of the family according to two or more modes of assessments studied in class, (b) a comparison of the family in the novel with our own family using the selected modes of assessment, and (c) an analysis of both families with regard to larger contextual issues such as gender, social class, culture, and race. This exercise not only encouraged me to engage in the world beyond family therapy, but also introduced me to a kind of life completely different from mine. I chose D. H. Lawrence's novel "*Sons and Lovers.*" I intentionally chose an author I did not know anything about, from a completely different ethnic and class background, to challenge my own stereotypes and to understand the novel within its own historical context.

This kind of exercise helped me establish: (a) a historical perspective on the evolution of my family and the novel's family, (b) an analysis of the structural constraints playing a role in the relationships of dominance by class and gender, and (c) an analysis of the individual possibilities for change within each family.

This exercise required both group and individual work, since it combined a search at both the individual/family level and the theoretical level. The work format included coaching groups that were designed to support people both in terms of the analysis and the personal challenges that might arise during the particular searches that each of us did. My group was composed of three women: Cheng, from Japan; Pamela, from the West Indies; and myself. Again, we joined in the endeavor of making sense out of our differing backgrounds and the theories we were studying. The group work was usually included in the format of our projects, even if the final paper was individual. Through the process of working together with people from different backgrounds we had to learn: (a) how to be relevant to one another in equitable terms, that is, how to connect so that we could develop a collaborative relation to negotiate meanings about the materials studied, (b) how to contextualize the theory so that it spoke to us in relation to our previous and present work environments, and (c) how to reconstruct aspects of our personal stories.

ADDRESSING SILENCE
FROM A NARRATIVE PERSPECTIVE

I chose to develop my ideas about family therapy training from a narrative perspective because it offered me a framework to articulate my personal experience with gender and culture issues at the level of social discourse. The narrative perspective opened a space for understanding the dynamics of silencing through the imposition of discourses that constrain me as a woman coming from Latin America.

I experienced a shift from a context in which I was privileged by my socioeconomic background and education—though certainly not by my condition as a woman—to a context in which I was constantly identified as a "minority." I also experienced a shift from a context in which my childhood household included my maternal grandmother, great-aunt, uncle, parents, and brothers to a context in which the nuclear family composition has a privileged, normative status. Somehow, most of the people who are part of the dominant ethnic culture "assign me" an identity based on their views/experiences of Spanish-speaking people in this country, without ever questioning where I "really" come from. Resisting the consistent challenge of discourses which attempt to constrain some of my possibilities as a human being, by determining what is appropriate for me as a woman of my age or from me as "minority," has become an essential part of my struggle to find approaches to therapy that address the common concerns that I share with so many people from "Third World" countries.

Those aspects of feminist thinking which have developed narrative approaches (Hare-Mustin, 1978; Kliman, 1995; Roberts, 1994; Weingarten, 1991) offer tools to address issues that challenge patriarchal practices, as well as to open space to many other contexts, such as my own (the political struggle in Latin America). In the educational arena, narrative and feminist approaches offer key possibilities to prevent the silencing of students coming from a nondominant culture in the U.S., because they: (a) locate us and our stories in space and time, (b) address our experiences (oral and written) as a social account (as opposed to an intrapsychic concept), (c) analyze the contextual possibilities and constraints of a situation, and (d) locate and challenge the positioning of stories in terms of dominance.

From my perspective this creates an environment that addresses the educational experience at the levels of: (a) the individual and community's context, (b) the value of the theories and tools studied in family therapy, and (c) the process in which learning occurs.

POSTSCRIPT.
AUTOBIOGRAPHICAL DISCONTINUITIES:
A "KIND" OF ADJUSTING TO LIVING
IN DIFFERENT CULTURES

A final theme I will address is the inevitable experience of cultural dislocation. This occurred for me when I went back home for several months after three years abroad. While in Bogota, I was a consultant for a progressive Catholic organization that develops retreat programs for high schools in the city. This organization was interested in finding ways to respond to the challenges that youths were facing in light of the dramatically increased divorce rate in the last few years. We agreed to work based on a Freirian framework (1971) within which we developed the contents for the workshop activities by having the students as primary participants in the process. We collectively aimed to understand their concerns and transform them.

However, our agreement to let the students serve as primary informants did not always happen. In fact, I realized the very thin line between working with persons as subjects who know and act and treating persons as objects who are known and acted upon (Freire, 1971; Korin, 1994; Mirkin, 1990). For example, while I was concerned with gendered views about family roles that place women in unequal situations that reinforce inequality even more after divorce and the effects of such situations on children, other participants were more concerned about the importance of the "saving face" dynamic in a society where divorce is still stigmatized. Still others were concerned about the "psychologically devastating effects" of divorce on children. During the process of negotiating our priorities and strategies for approaching the issues, I stood back to observe myself in an intense situation of adjusting to a new context. Even though I anticipated that it would take time to overcome some challenges in re-adapting to Bogota's context, the actual experience involved a practice of learning how the meaning of my words/actions were validated or invalidated according to the different rules arising from varying social contexts.

On the one hand, I struggled between staying at the level of a local, context-specific definition of the issues and strategies in this program; and on the other hand, staying at the level of legitimizing an agenda based on an outside logic. So too, I struggled with feelings of confusion, and a sense of not belonging at the same time. Pondering the dangers of reproducing a colonial and patronizing attitude in the consultation, my eventual choice was to find criteria of validity within the context, expecting that the process of "problematizing" would open a space to design a program relevant to its recipients.

This experience produced yet another layer of complexity to the already intricate maze of cultural transitions involved. "Narrativizing" has been the major path that I have followed to make sense of my past and present. The discontinuities that I perceive in my lifetime, the dislocations, have the possibility of being woven together in narratives as I elaborate on them with other people. This maze of changes and transitions is a never ending set of experiences, accounts, and interpretations. Narratives provide a "map" since they are constructed in the context of social interactions, and allow a continuous adjustment of socially constructed subjectivity. Narrativizing of this kind captures the shifting subjectivities, always seen in their social context, and helps in recognizing others' subjectivities in the context of their own historical and social determinants. In my life and in my feminist, family therapy training, narrative work has emerged as an effective tool for making sense of the contradictions of personal experience and social context.

REFERENCES

Freire, P. (1971). *The pedagogy of the oppressed*. New York: Herder and Herder.

Hare-Mustin, R. (1978). *A feminist approach to family therapy*. Family Process, *17*, 181-194.

Kliman, J. (1995). The interweaving of gender, class and race in family therapy. In M.P. Mirkin (Ed.), *Women in context*, (pp. 25-47). New York: The Guilford Press.

Korin, E.C. (1994). Social inequalities and therapeutic relationships: Applying Freire's ideas to clinical practice. In R.V. Almeida, *Expansions of family therapy through diversity*. New York: The Haworth Press, Inc.

Mirkin, M.P. (1990). *The social and political contexts of family therapy.* Boston: Allyn and Bacon.

Roberts, J. (1994). *Tales and transformations: Stories in families and family therapy.* New York: Norton.

Santamaria, M.C. (1990). Couples therapy: Analysis of a "praxis" with a freirian perspective. *Family Process, 29* (2), 119-129.

Weingarten, K. (1991). The discourses of intimacy: Adding a social constructionist and feminist view. *Family Process, 30,* 285-305.

A View from Europe:
Gender in Training and Continuing Education
of Family Therapists

Rosmarie Welter-Enderlin

SUMMARY. The author presents an overview of training in gender-informed family therapy in six Central European countries based on responses from 12 teachers of family therapy. The respondents show that the gender topic is an important part of training in their progressive institutions. However, as one colleague writes, the leadership of the "official" European organizations and associations is still "totally male-oriented." Though the respondents to the "gender in training" survey offer a variety of teaching techniques, they believe that the best way to sensitize students to the gender issue is to make their family of origin experience a core aspect of training. *[Article copies available from The Haworth Document Delivery Service: 1-800-342-9678. E-mail address: getinfo@haworth.com]*

I was both excited and embarrassed by the request by the editors of this volume to contribute a paper to an issue on training in

Rosmarie Welter-Enderlin, MSW, social scientist, family therapist and organizational counselor, is Director, Training Institute for Systemic Therapy and Counseling (Ausbildungsinstitut), Meilen/Zurich, and Lecturer in Psychology, U of Zurich.

Address correspondence to Dorfstrasse 94, CH-8706 Meilen/Zurich.

The author would like to thank Michele Bograd and Kathy Weingarten, as well as Evan Imber-Black for their assistance in editing this paper.

[Haworth co-indexing entry note]: "A View from Europe: Gender in Training and Continuing Education of Family Therapists." Welter-Enderlin, Rosmarie. Co-published simultaneously in *Journal of Feminist Family Therapy* (The Haworth Press, Inc.) Vol. 8, No. 2, 1996, pp. 53-74; and: *Reflections on Feminist Family Therapy Training* (ed: Kathy Weingarten, and Michele Bograd) The Haworth Press, Inc., 1996, pp. 53-74. Single or multiple copies of this article are available from The Haworth Document Delivery Service [1-800-342-9678, 9:00 a.m. - 5:00 p.m. (EST). E-mail address: getinfo@haworth.com].

feminist therapy in Europe. The excitement relates to the fact that in the past 12 years, this topic has been one of the major challenges in my work as a teacher and practitioner of family therapy. In 1986, my feminist writing and networking with five prominent female colleagues was a major reason for losing my acceptability in a patriarchal training and therapy institution. The experience infuriated me enough to found an alternative institution, which I did with a group of female and male colleagues. We have been teaching and writing as a group for the past 8 years now, and our private nonprofit training Meilen/Zurich Institute in Switzerland is flourishing. In fact, we receive so many applications for basic training in gender-informed systemic therapy annually that we are able to put together groups of 12 women and 12 men from the fields of psychology, social work, and medicine for each of the two years in our training programs.

As I pondered the term "Europe" in the editors' request, however, I felt embarrassed. Europe? I am aware of family therapy developments in only a few European countries. In fact, I know less and less where Europe lies. Russia is part of it, is it not?–and so is the former Yugoslavia. But I know little or nothing about family therapy in those countries, let alone about training. There may not be much of it going on there these days, considering their political situation. But, then, I don't really know.

The field of family therapy is well developed and has become mainstream in the parts of Europe I am familiar with, consisting of Great Britain, the Scandinavian countries, Austria, Belgium, Germany, France, Holland, Italy, and Switzerland. Most of the training is done in private institutes whose members often teach graduate classes at universities, e.g., in the Departments of Psychiatry, Family Medicine, and Psychology, or at Schools of Social Work. One of the five colleagues at our private Meilen/Zurich Institute is a full professor of sociology in Jena/Germany, while I teach family therapy in the context of graduate psychology at the University of Zurich. Many of my graduate students later apply for the two-year training course in systemic therapy at our institute. In regard to practice, one striking difference is that while in Switzerland family therapy is an important part of inpatient and outpatient psychiatry, this is not so anymore in Germany. There, family therapy is part of most community and private agencies serving children, young adults, couples, and families. One of the differences between Germany and Switzerland is that at the Institute in Meilen/Zurich, we receive as many applications from resident psychiatrists (supported by their institutions) as from people in other contexts. This means that in contrast to Germany, family therapy is done here by as many male as female professionals with basic training in psychology, social work, psychiatry, and family medicine. While I notice at conferences and seminars in Germany a ratio of two-thirds women and one-third men, most of the conferences and seminars offered in Switzerland attract about an equal number of women and men. Also, male teachers of family therapy predominate in Germany but to a lesser extent in Switzerland and Austria. However, when it comes to specific gender themes or when, for instance, two women are teaching a course, male participants tend to stay away in all the European countries I know. This raises the question of how to have gender-informed training in family therapy that can attract qualified men and women, resulting in women feeling equally empowered to raise their voices in the larger social context. Personally, I tend to co-teach seminars with male and female colleagues as often as possible. This is but a first step in changing a social context that does not take women's voices as seriously as men's.

I am aware of a tremendous interest in family/systemic therapy in Eastern Europe (e.g., Czechoslovakia, Hungary, Poland), especially in regard to social psychiatry and couples therapy. Each encounter with colleagues from the Eastern part of Europe confirms my impression, however, that they have strong reservations regarding the possible "colonialization" through concepts of families and family therapy which have been developed in Western contexts. Some of these colleagues tell me that after the fall of the iron curtain five years ago, the influx of well-meaning American and western European colleagues has convinced them that they will need to develop their own concepts, however important their exchange with Western theory building may be.

The most discussed question in the central European family therapy circles these days is whether the field should advance in the direction of a "general approach to therapy" rather than the known specialization on couples and families. Most of the training institutes (ours included) therefore prefer the term "systemic counseling and therapy," indicating that our focus is not a specific group of clients but a certain mode of understanding and assisting human beings within their sociobiological and historical contexts. For the past few years, every major conference in the German-speaking parts of Europe has dedicated about one-fourth of the official time to the organization of research on the efficacy of systemic family therapy as well as on its acceptance by the health insurance systems. The German equivalent of AFTA, a professional organization named DAF, has initiated a nationwide outcome research program in which many training and therapy institutions participate. The professional organizations of family/systemic therapy in Austria, Germany, and Switzerland have been making great efforts toward the goal of becoming the third major concept of therapy (besides the already privileged concepts of psychoanalysis and socio-behavior modification) in their respective countries. Austria's professional organization has succeeded in including systemic therapy (offered also by nonmedical but specifically trained professionals) in their new psychotherapy law, but is now meeting with tough resistance by the medical lobby. The German and Swiss professional organizations of systemic/family therapy are still working hard to be included in the pending public regulation of psychotherapy.

As a consequence of my lack of familiarity with Europe as a whole, I decided to focus my task by calling upon my personal network of colleagues in a few central European countries. This, of course, means that most of the persons I addressed are in some ways related to a major concern we represent at our institute, i.e., sensitivity to the sociocultural as well as political contexts of therapy. In regard to gender issues, however, the replies to my questions will show some interesting differences. In the spring of 1995, I put together a list of several questions with regard to gender in the training and continuing education of family therapists and sent it to 35 colleagues in nine European countries. Seven women and five men from six countries whose addresses are listed at the end of this paper answered. There are two man/woman couples among them, one married, the other professional associates. The absence of answers from my Scandinavian and Dutch colleagues surprised me. Many of them have participated in the first international conference on "Women and Family Therapy" (1991) in Copenhagen, organized by a group of American family therapists, which attracted close to 90 colleagues from 27 countries. There are many small but influential feminist family therapy networks in Europe which were strongly supported by the Copenhagen conference. However, once again language and culture account for regional rather than European communities. Since the Copenhagen meeting, for instance, there have been two conferences on the gender perspective for female family therapists in Germany, and a third one is planned in the spring of 1996. More than 200 experienced professionals from Germany, Austria, and Switzerland have attended these conferences, and there is a growing interest among younger women. I can speculate why only relatively few answered my questions. Perhaps the gender topic has become so much of their everyday practice that it is not worth writing about it in a general way. Rather, specific questions like "How does a gender informed perspective apply to therapeutic language, to family violence, working with men, to eating disorders, etc.?" seem to interest the colleagues I have asked.

Let me now list the respondents by country (see end of article for their full addresses). I will use their first names in the text, although in the central part of Europe we tend to do so only with close friends. From Austria, Rudi Kronbichler; from Germany, Margaret Hecker, Ingeborg Ruecker-Embden-Jonasch, Gunthard Weber, Gisal and Werner Wnuk-Gette; from Italy, Matteo Selvini; from Poland, Maria Orwid; from Switzerland, Elisabeth Fivas-Deupeursinge, and Beatrice Olbert and Josef Haenggi; and from Wales, Philippa Seligman.

I will add pertinent information from the perspective of our training group in Meilen as well. Their names also appear at the end of this paper. As I have to translate most texts from German, some shades of meaning may be missing, as may be true for other responses written in English as the non-primary language.

Question 1: Does gender play a role in your teaching and supervision? In what ways?

Not surprisingly, the women in my sample tend to be more identified with making gender a specific topic of their teaching than some of the men. Many of those asked did not bother to reply. There are exceptions among male trainers however, who specify how they have overcome their former gender-blindness. Also, interesting references to a certain fatigue in regard to the gender topic in some former socialist countries were made by two female respondents.

Let me begin with Philippa Seligman from Great Britain. She writes, "Gender has a very high priority in my clinical practice of family therapy and in my teaching/training practice. Students are encouraged to develop a high awareness of the significance of gender roles and beliefs in every aspect of their work. This would include asking clients what differences they might perceive in having a male or female therapist as well as eliciting patterns within their social contexts."

All respondents, with the exception of Maria from Poland and Gunthard from Heidelberg, write that the gender topic is a central and official part of their teaching. Maria indicates that she is not concerned directly with gender in her teaching "but I think I am overloading women and in some way protecting men, regarding them as the weaker and more vulnerable of human beings." At the end of the questionnaire, Maria "promises to think more about the gender issue." Gunthard indicates that he does not put the gender topic on his teaching banner. "Officially, it hardly emerges in connection with my name," he writes. "The gender theme is promoted by Andrea and Ingeborg (the two women in the Heidelberg team). However, as I become more aware of gendered stories, I pay more attention to the topic than five to ten years ago." Gunthard's colleague Ingeborg writes that she wants gender issues to be a central part of teaching and therapeutic practice, "not a topic to be mentioned once and then forget it."

Another German colleague, Gisal, indicates that she and her husband Werner have been teaching and doing therapy as a married couple since 1978. However, only in the past five years have publications on feminist family therapy encouraged them to become more systematically involved in teaching this perspective. American feminist family therapists seem to play an important part in sensitizing many of the respondents to gender issues. Gisal and other respondents, for instance Rudi, say they owe a great deal to the writings of Imber Black and McGoldrick, among others like

John Gottman (referred to by Elisabeth) who are known in Europe. One of the most often cited American influences is the Women's Project (Carter, Silverstein, Papp and Walters) and their book *The Invisible Web* which was translated into German soon after its appearance. In the past ten years, an impressive body of gender-related literature in German has appeared in the field of systemic family therapy. Some major titles are mentioned in the bibliography. For European male trainers, it seems important to refer to writings by other men. Rudi, for instance, notes that he likes to use Karl Tomm's notion of "internalized other interviewing" to teach about gender differences in order to gain alternative descriptions of the world by women and men. There seems to be a gender difference in how European family therapy trainers apply certain ideas to teaching about gender, which is represented in the ways by which they use the terms reality versus construction of reality. My personal impression is that the term "description of the world," used by Rudi, tends to imply freedom of choice, a notion particularly cherished by many of my European male colleagues who seem fascinated by the idea of changing the world by "languaging" alternatives. None of my women colleagues refers to this brand of constructivism in their response. Rather, as we do at the Meilen Institute, we assume that any description of the world is firmly anchored in a specific reality, i.e., that there are rather narrow opportunities for the "invention" and change of a particular world by the use of language.

Interesting and very European to me is the fact that especially my women respondents write about paying a great deal of attention to local contexts by teaching social and political history in their family therapy training. There is still a great variety among geographical and ethnic milieus in the central parts of Europe which is present in local dialects, customs, rituals, and norms. Beatrice, who teaches in the highly industrialized Basel region (which borders on rural France and Germany), writes about going back 150 years to the time of regional industrialization with her trainees. She encourages them, for instance, to study the trajectories of young rural women who had to work in silk weaving factories from early childhood and witnessed their urban peers' rebellion and subsequent incarceration. The implicit message of such studies is that there has been repression of women, but also rebellion, earlier in history. Beatrice also tells her trainees about typical local marital patterns of the 19th century and how rebellious women were pathologized by husbands and medical doctors, making sure her students understand how the personal always was and is political. The reflection of social history is linked by many trainers to survival strategies of women, e.g., symptoms like depression or "hysteria," which are understood more from a societal than an intrapsychic perspective.

At the Meilen Institute we teach students how to go beyond the "factual" information in their own and their clients' genograms by putting the "facts" into the sociopolitical context of the time when important decisions in the family of origin were made. Specifically, we ask questions about the options and limitations individual women and men had in their milieu at specific points in time, and why they took this or another course of action. Quite often, theirs was not a voluntary decision but the only possible response to the prevailing social circumstances and the structures of meaning a particular family generated from them. According to the Meilen concept, we teach students always to connect a specific family story and its structures of meaning with the possibilities and limitations of individual women or men at a certain time in a certain place.

A fascinating example of how the historical and the personal merge is provided by Margaret in the former East German Democratic Republic (GDR). She writes: "It is very difficult to raise the gender topic with female colleagues who have been socialized in that context. They tend to feel that Westerners do not consider them as 'real women' when it comes to their involvement with family and economy under socialism. These women demand a great deal from themselves, especially now that many of their spouses are out of work. Only gradually do they realize that it is too much for them." The term feminism seems to be loaded in some former socialist countries in ways I did not realize before, as Margaret's and Maria's replies indicate. In my search for explanations, I found Eva Hoffman's (1993) report on her recent experience of Eastern Europe. On page 80 (op. cit.), Hoffman explains the reluctance by East European women, particularly Polish women, to be identified as feminists as follows: "Feminism, insofar as it exists here, is a target of reflexive scorn or disapproval. For one thing, like socialism, feminism was co-opted and corrupted by its association with official ideology. . . . But it is clear from their conversation that the feminine dilemma here is interestingly different from the American situation. In some ways, they are starting from a rather more advanced point—that is, if we envision history as a progress toward our notions of progress. For one thing, Poland never went through an equivalent of the American fifties, with the cult of domesticity and suburban isolation. Under the Communist dispensations, women were expected to work, and they did, in nearly the same proportions as the men. Higher education was more discriminatory by class than gender—discriminatory, that is, against the upper classes—and women entered the professions in relatively large numbers, and reached high levels of authority, if rarely the highest." It becomes obvious then that one of the indispensable clues to understanding European differences in family therapy training and practice, as well as the importance or non-importance of gender issues, lies in the regional and historical complexities.

An interesting reference to the revision of the history of central ideas in family therapy in Europe is made by Matteo Selvini of Milan. He is Mara Selvini Palazzoli's son, but is clearly differentiating from her ideas and working methods. While his mother never seemed to pay much attention to gender issues, in fact, has been criticized by feminist family therapists in regard to her "gender-blindness," Matteo writes:

> In our training activity we are concerned with changing the 'old' systemic way of thinking which tends to minimize the differences between family members by employing 'collective' hypotheses and a 'neutral' approach. Our students need to learn of the existence of psychologically as well as socially determined conflicts of interest in the family. Gender differences are a basic source of a socially determined conflict of interests in the family. The family therapist cannot be neutral. He/she has to start from a position of alliance with the women in the family (parallel to the alliance with the patient who suffers from a psychologically determined conflict of interest). Recently, the gender theme has become important in our investigation about the family process in anorexia. I was dis-

turbed to discover our former bias against mothers, even in our latest book. Our future publication on anorexia will feature an important change, also from this point of view. Italian family therapy nearly always ignores the gender-theme. Our 'official' leadership is totally male, and many of the few women (leaders) do not contribute positively, either because of the limits of their contributions, or–and most important–because they obtain 'visibility' *only* as the wife of some important man.

I have given ample space to the replies to my first question in order to reflect the state of the art of feminist family therapy in some major central European teaching contexts. However, as my network of colleagues is biased in favor of nonsexist teaching, this is in no way an adequate representation of the current trends. In fact, I am convinced from attending various conferences organized by the European Family Therapy Association (EFTA) that Matteo's information on the Italian family therapy scene pertains to most other European countries as well. With some exceptions where women and men work together at the same hierarchical level (as, for instance, at the Institutes in Basel, Lausanne, and Meilen/Switzerland), or Philippa Seligman and Marie-Louise Conen who teach in their own institutes (in Wales and in Berlin), family therapy training in Europe remains dominated by men. Most often, they are anchored in psychiatry and are either MDs or derive status from the medical field. European conferences on family therapy usually reflect this trend, with few exceptions. If women are invited on stage, it is "acceptable" that they are not MDs, provided they are flown in from the USA or have been trained there. The prophetesses seem to account for little in their own land.

Question 2: When I think of my experience, what special situations/ stories in teaching and supervision come to my mind?

Again, an interesting gender difference becomes visible. Female trainers tend to reflect upon the social context of their students and clients and on how to enhance trainees' sensitivity to it, while male trainers tend to write about teaching techniques. I consider both, of course, to be important aspects of training and practice, but find the gendered work division between reflecting and doing rather disturbing. I am sadly familiar with this situation, especially in male-directed European training institutes which write "solution oriented systemic therapy" on their banner and largely ignore social context and gender.

Let me now turn to the replies to my question: Margaret, teaching in Eastern Germany, refers to the gender differences in her students' families of origin. Daughters now in training for social work have typically played second fiddle at home. "All family efforts would be concentrated on the higher education of the only son," Margaret writes, "who then failed school. The daughter, even though doing well, had to leave school to help her family and her brother. Only later in life, through adult education in social work, has she finally been able to use her talents and become a professional." Margaret reflects upon the importance of helping these women to resolve their guilt feelings for having "betrayed" their families' ideals by becoming more successful than their brothers.

Beatrice observes in her teaching how often male trainees are convinced that they lead a perfectly egalitarian couple relationship, a conviction that is seriously shaken when the group is taught to operationalize gender equality in terms of specific daily actions and the allocation of power. Ingeborg regrets the fact that since she has achieved a reputation as a feminist family therapist, male trainees seem to prefer seminars by her male colleagues. The few men who "by accident" make it to her courses, she observes, appear at first sight softer and less "full of themselves" than others. However, she writes, they usually experience positive regard for their maleness by the women in the course and, if there are enough of them, engage in a fervent but constructive gender-discourse. "If there are very few men, however, they tend to withdraw from the sometimes over-generalized and even destructive gender-discussion among women, which is why I prefer a more equal balance," Ingeborg writes. The central issue in the male-female conflicts experienced here sees power as created by societal stereotypes (Hare-Mustin & Marecek, 1990). When women represent the majority and men are in the minority, as often happens in Ingeborg's seminars, the tensions between them clearly do not refer to their basic sexual or behavioral differences but to a context in which the societal expectations and habitual positions of the sexes in the power hierarchies are reversed.

As such reversals often happen in family therapy practice and training, I have learned to put the emerging tension between male and female trainees (or spouses), into the dominant societal discourse. By doing so, I depathologize women's "letting men have it" as well as men's sarcasm or defensiveness vis-à-vis the "dominant women." In fact, the reversal of the habitual societal positions of men and women in family therapy training often results in anger but also in laughter at the absurdity of the situation, thus reaching the trainees' gut level far better than cognitive information only. In a similar way, Gisal and especially Werner observe how often very competent women yield the right of way to "weaker" men in seminars and are then laughingly provoked by the trainers to realize what they are doing. In my experience, the reversed fairy tale of the "Frog-Prince," in which the overprotected frogs never become princes, is a good metaphor to use when male trainees complain about the provocations by female colleagues.

Philippa answers my question by writing that "in the U.K., the Association for Family Therapy sets criteria for training courses and there is a requirement for courses to give a positive and prominent status to gender awareness as part of an anti-oppressive practice stance." Matteo states: "We have not developed special training activities, aside from the organization of special seminars on ethics and family therapy where gender and other political problems are the main topic." The techniques reported by Gunthard and Rudi to enhance gender sensitivity will be summarized later in this paper.

Question 3: What is my personal definition of "non-sexist" therapy and teaching?

Being aware of the generally negative connotation of the term "feminism" not only in Eastern Europe but also in the German-speaking part of Europe, I referred to "non-sexist" practice in my questionnaire. The question was generally not liked by my male respondents who felt it was quite guilt-inducing.

Gunthard: "In the first place, I do not like the term (non-sexist therapy). I prefer the teaching of systems therapy to be based on ideas and processes which support men as well as women in their right to egalitarian access to resources and political decisions, while conserving their identity as men and women. Equality and mutual respect enhance all areas of life, including that of sexuality." I guess this is exactly what we mean by feminist or non-sexist therapy, is it not? Rudi informs us that in his opinion, non-sexist therapy "prefers descriptions and explanations which include the experience of both women and men." He gives much credit to the women authors in the field for widening his perspectives and for learning about "differences that make a difference in the therapeutic potential."

To Elisabeth, non-sexist therapy is "always to keep in touch with the other gender." Beatrice comments that she and her male colleagues no longer assume that non-sexist teaching means that men and women should perform exactly the same way or do the same tasks, but that their contributions must be negotiable. Most important to them is that men learn to pay attention to the position of women in social hierarchies and to the underlying operative value systems. Ingeborg wants students to practice specifically how to talk about gender differences with their clients and to connect their individual experiences with the larger context, e.g., by saying "most women suffer from insecurity when they go back to work after many years in the family."

At the Meilen Institute we find it helpful to teach students that gendered language is related to power positions in the context of marriage, family, and institutions, i.e., if women talk in a relational way and men in a positional way, it is not because they are better or worse human beings, but because of their one-down or one-up situation in a specific context. It seems helpful that most of our students are aware of Hegel's dialectics of master-servant relations to understand how positions of power between men and women are related to the asymmetrical allocation of resources in society. We insist that our students learn to identify the different power sources (or lack thereof) of women and men, girls and boys in various social contexts. And we assume, as do Gisal and Werner, that one of the most potent ways of teaching what non-sexist cooperation means is to demonstrate an egalitarian co-teaching model between men and women. Trainees report that the sophisticated yet lusty exchange of ideas and contradictions between female and male trainers greatly enhance their courage openly to deal with gender issues in their personal lives as well as with clients.

*Question 4: Which specific procedures and techniques do I use or
have I developed in order to teach trainees to become aware and cope
with gender issues?*

A wealth of information was offered to me in reply to this question. There seems to be a consensus among male and female respondents that the reconstruction of the trainee's family of origin in regard to gendered roles and rituals over generations is a most powerful means of learning about gender in connection with historical, ethnic, and regional conditions.

Let me now present the major procedure the Meilen team uses to sensitize trainees to the social, cultural, and gender aspects of their family of origin and of client families in various milieus. In the first stage of our two-year training course, each student is handed a semi-structured list of questions pertaining to three generations of their personal genogram. Trainees are encouraged to start a diary on "My family and myself," beginning with any one of the questions that seem exciting or relevant at the time. One of the chosen questions might be, for instance: "In what ways is my current situation similar/different from the same-sex parent when he or she was my age? What did he or she have to cope with at that stage of life?" Another question requires the drawing of a floor plan of the apartment in which the trainee spent the longest period with his or her family. The trainee is then asked to delineate the private spheres of father, mother, and of each of the children, even if they consisted only of a private drawer or closet space. Quite often, it becomes obvious immediately that the women in the family had no room of their own at all, while father and the boys owned work space in the basement, private desks, or at least a regular chair in the local pub. Each student works privately on the approximately 20 questions throughout the first year of training, consulting important members of his or her family of origin and collecting old letters and pictures to answer newly raised questions.

At the end of the first year of training, the 24 trainees and their five trainers/supervisors gather for a week in a small hotel in the Southern Alps. The topic of this week is the reconstruction of family themes and leitmotifs and how they affect each person's life and therapeutic practice. In the intimacy of the supervision groups led by the supervisor of the first year, half of the week is spent exploring students' experiences in reconstructing their family of origin. We look at photographs and objects, we ask questions and help each trainee weave the threads of his or her life into a tapestry combining old and newly recovered family themes. Special attention is paid to the trainees' roles as a daddy's girl or boy, or mommy's girl or boy, and what it means if they have not yet accepted being part of the more distant (and often less powerful) parent's story. In the opening plenary, I usually present a personal videotape showing my interviews with my mother's only surviving sister in search of my mother's almost unknown story. One day of this week is spent with a local anthropologist exploring the various ways in which gender issues are expressed in this conservative Catholic rural region, e.g., by analyzing differences in male/female obituaries. In the second half of the week, we use the matrix of each trainee's personal experience to look at one case he or she brought into supervision during the first year, and how it affected their joys or sorrows with that family. As an example, during live supervision in the first year, a woman school psychologist got into serious trouble with the emotional distancing of the divorced father of a young girl. Looking back, she recognized how she pursued this man "as if he were my father," a politician who maintained a façade of the intact family but had never been available to his daughter.

The second year of training is deeply affected by the experience of this week and we observe a much greater mutual openness in regard to gender, power, and personal history than before. I often notice that male trainees who kept me at arm's length during supervision in the first year whenever I raised aspects of gender or power become much more open to these topics after having become involved with their mother's stories.

To return to the replies I received from my colleagues, Rudi refers to the "Meal-Ritual Exercises" he learned from the training and writings of Imber-Black et al. (1988). The question "What gender rules were expressed via shopping, cooking, serving, talking, cleaning up?" he writes, is an excellent starter for dealing with the gender question in training groups. Also, he refers to Rambo et al.'s (1993) exercise number 19, "Retell the Story of Cinderella," and Sheinberg and Penn's "Gender Questions" (1991) as well as

White's (1992) exercise of "challenging and deconstructing biases about the essentialist nature of men and women."

Gunthard prefers storytelling when teaching about gender. He recounts, for instance, a workshop with Olga Silverstein in which he role-played the husband, and how he expected the trainer "to fix" the generational boundaries and was perplexed when Olga called forth the women's solidarity across generations. Also, Gunthard tells his trainees stories of gendered experiences in his family of origin. His father's mother was one of ten children. Only her brothers were allowed to go to the University while the sisters did not even receive enough money to get married. Of particular interest to him, as to all German respondents, is how the Second World War affected the relations between women and men (Gunthard's parents were separated for 11 years). In addition to stories, Gunthard uses the gender questions presented in Heidelberg by Virginia Goldner and Evan Imber Black (op. cit.) as well as my work on typical male and female talk in relation to power positions (Welter-Enderlin, 1992). Gunthard encourages students to look at gendered elements of rituals in their daily lives. His "specialty" is the reconstruction of at least two generations of the trainees' family of origin, a family sculpture exercise which shows specific bonding and distancing patterns in regard to couples as well as parents and children. Gunthard writes that he increasingly conducts workshops together with a woman colleague and invites more women to teach in his training courses than before. "The difference of how women open up to female trainers in contrast to male trainers never ceases to surprise me," he observes.

Among the exercises used by most respondents are reversed role-plays between men and women. For instance, they reverse male/female dialogues recorded in family therapy or at political meetings. "If it sounds funny or absurd when you reverse it, you can be sure that the talk is sexist" is one of the principles. The polarization of the dominant societal gender discourse and listening to its absurdities (e.g., "the psyche of women and men is radically different in the following ways . . .") is mentioned by many trainers of family therapy. Ingeborg uses role reversal exercises to teach trainees what it means for women to be subsumed in texts using only the male form of language. This is a particular problem in German as the nouns are gendered, for instance, in the word therapist or client. We may either use the male or female form, but most often, of course, only the male form is applied. A very important exercise, Ingeborg writes, is the analysis of language in diagnostic and therapeutic records and how often it creates realities that disadvantage women and girls. It should be noted that there is no word for "gender" in German and that either the English term is used or its meaning is circumscribed in German.

Commercial videotapes and films are often used as a basis for role reversal exercises, especially in order to analyze the differences in verbal and nonverbal communication between spouses, writes Elisabeth. Margaret developed a similar exercise through which trainees "find the implicit gender biases over four generations in their family of origin." She suggests it be done in pairs of female and male trainees.

Gisal and Werner also pay a great deal of attention to gender-biased language but more to written than oral language, it being obvious that talking becomes more complicated than writing if you insist on changing old habits. Early in the training of family therapists, they do the following exercise: They ask each trainee to choose three partners of the opposite sex. In a process lasting several hours, the pairs intermittently engage in a dialogue on the following questions: (a) What do I appreciate in you as a woman (or a man)? (b) What makes it difficult for me to like you as a woman (or a man)? (c) What aspects of you as a woman (or a man) would I like to be more visible?

Question 5: What kinds of consequences of my teaching do I observe? How do my male and female trainees use their awareness and possible techniques in regard to gender in their own practice?

Question 6: In what ways do I consider the gender theme in the European Family Therapy "scene" to be handled constructively or unconstructively?

Since questions 5 and 6 are related, I will summarize their responses together. All respondents write that mostly positive consequences result when gender is made a central aspect of teaching. But the consequences have a different impact depending on the sex and the generation of the cohort.

Gisal and Werner differentiate four distinct groups of trainees. The first group is women trainees around or above age 40 who usually have raised children and are curious and eager to discuss the topic and translate their insights into daily practice. The second group is male trainees around or above age 40. They frequently react with anger or guilt to the gender topic, Gisal and Werner observe, as many of them have spouses who gave up their careers in order to support that of their husband. Sometimes, together with a female co-therapist (especially if she is experienced), they open up and become sensitive to the gender question. The third group is comprised of female trainees between 35 and 40 who often are experienced in women's groups. They seem to be the group most curious and ready to translate gender topics into their daily practice. Last is the subset of male trainees between 35 and 40. In Gisal and Werner's view, they are usually quite sensitive to gender questions, having participated in men's groups. These men impress their trainers as particularly careful in avoiding any "macho" behaviors, thus sometimes renouncing a certain "bite" or provoking stance in therapy. In co-therapy with an experienced (female) colleague, they apparently regain their bite, the trainers note. Rudi reports a similar observation. "The gender topic" he notes, "is at first the women's topic. Only gradually do the (fewer) male trainees engage more in gender discourse. Some of them later report what a difference it made for their practice, but also for their personal lives."

Margaret thoughtfully comments on her experience in a multi-professional teaching team. "Misconceptions are built in," she writes. "Men often become very defensive when the gender question is raised. Women tend to be disqualified by men in the teaching team, professionally as well as personally. The request to hire more female teachers of social work (where most students are female) is usually responded to by a power-oriented vote." One of the consequences of Margaret's careful dealing with gender questions is that female and male trainees now insist on involving fathers when there are family conflicts. Also, in public agencies they try to involve male and female workers in co-counseling. This is due to the sad fact that female social workers often are battered by male clients "who are extremely frustrated by their new situation on the labor market in the former Eastern Germany." Male directors of agencies insist, for instance, that women social workers take night duty which requires police protection. Whereas women trainees feel supported by feminist course content, Margaret writes, male trainees often cut her course, indicating that "enough is enough."

Beatrice also relates reluctance by male trainees to deal with the "female question" but feels that women's awakening and training in gender sensitivity has made an important difference in the European scene of family therapy. She critically notes, however, that while men in the field lag behind in regard to the consequences of gender discrimination, there are still too many women who accept things as they are. Gunthard observes that quite often, in his extended training courses, sensitivity to the discrimination of women grows. He observes a certain, sometimes humorous, "war between the sexes" attitude in his seminars where men easily become defensive.

Ingeborg states that some of the women in the field of family therapy are still too ready to adapt "male speak" when they achieve a certain position. She finds, however, that, all in all, there is more attention being paid to a gender balance in presentations at conferences and seminars. Women's networks have certainly made some impact on the patriarchal structure of European family therapy. "It is obvious, by the way," Ingeborg writes, "that plenary contributions by women colleagues are usually far better prepared and more innovative than those of the well-known men in the field. Unfortunately, these women do not receive adequate positive feedback, and, if so, mostly from women and in private. The men in power seem to still prefer a strategy of sarcasm or other ha-ha reactions when the patriarchal principle in our field is challenged."

Question 7: How do trainers talk to students about the view that the private is political, and do they encourage them to become politically involved?

Let me first present the position of the Meilen team (Hildenbrand, in press) on the topic of training, therapy, and political involvement. Therapy as well as training is always political, we assume, inasmuch as we base our thinking and actions on the idea that individuals can only be understood if their situation in the larger context is taken into consideration. We insist, however, that the frameworks of therapy and political action need to be differentiated and that politically-informed therapy should not be confused with official political action. The goal of therapy being the enhancement of personal autonomy, we consider the postmodern stance of "everything goes in whatever context" to be anti-therapeutic. While our basic orientation includes the encouragement of clients and trainees to take political action if they so desire, it excludes suggestions of how and where to get involved.

My respondents largely share our position, although they take different positions regarding the term "neutrality." Rudi insists that from his "social-constructionist" perspective, it is necessary to challenge trainees' value orientations in order for them critically to evaluate their own actions and the actions of their trainers. Gunthard prefers "neutrality" in therapy but suggests to trainees that taking a position in public as well as engaging in (joint) political action is important. Margaret reports that in the former Eastern Germany, she often tutors female students who write dissertations with attention to the gender issue. As part of this effort, she addresses the fact that gender themes are not being accepted in the public discourse. Margaret writes, "I very carefully deal with the women's apprehension because their male professors do not give them any support." Maria, who also lives in a former socialist East European country, writes: "Yes, I talk to students that human beings are political. No, I do not encourage them to take political action." Having reflected on the historical and political differences between Eastern and Western Europe, the information offered by Margaret and Maria can now be better understood.

Ingeborg reflects on how the recognition of the importance of the sociopolitical context has changed her training. One consequence is that the questioning of the underlying assumptions of family systems theories as well as of power structures in the teaching and therapeutic contexts are now a salient part of her work. Happily, she adds that it is amazing how many young women now search and find role models of strong women in their personal genogram as well as in the colleagues and teachers available in their professional milieu.

CONCLUSION

The situation of training in family therapy in central Europe in many ways resembles that of the USA, it appears. However, there are marked differences. Most striking is the reluctance to even use the term feminism in Eastern Europe, but also in parts of the German-speaking Europe. Another difference from the U.S. is the general rootedness by students and clients in local and regional histories as well as their culture- and language-based identities. The ease by which individual genograms can be related to a certain continuity of general knowledge over generations also makes for important differences in family therapy and training. If trainees learn to pin the inner and outer aspects of family life by connecting individual stories with the sociocultural context of their personal family of origin, they tend to replace a possible keyhole perspective on their clients by a far broader understanding which naturally involves gender issues. In regionally "closed" milieus which still exist outside of urban areas in many parts of Europe, students have to learn how to deal with gender bias and social control issues, which often are not known in large cities. This seems to be the price for the stability of living in traditional communities.

Let me close on this positive note. Even though I am personally and professionally connected to most of my respondents, I have been surprised and impressed by the wealth of hitherto unknown information I received to my questions. A questionnaire like this might be a useful tool for others to investigate the current state of gender awareness in the training community. My impression is that many new aspects will emerge in the translation of our common feminist interests to teaching and therapy from asking similar questions in various sociocultural contexts.

ADDRESSES OF RESPONDENTS

Elisabeth Fivaz-Depeursinge, PhD, Professor, Research and Teaching Centre d'Etude de la Famille (CEF), Departement Universitaire de Psychiatrie Adulte Route de Cery, CH-1008 Prilly-Lausanne, Switzerland

Dr. Margaret Hecker, Professor of Social Work, Fachhochschule fur Sozialwesen, Kirchstrasse 15, D-64372 Ober-Ramstadt, Germany

Ingeborg Ruecker-Embdendonasch, Dipl.Psych. Mozartstr. 3, D-69121 Heidelberg, Germany

Maria Orwid, MD, Professor, The Jagiellonian University, Collegium Medicum, Dept. of Child and Adolescent Psychiatry, Kopernika 21 A, 31-501 Krakow, Poland
Philippa Seligman, Family Therapist, 22 West Orchard Crescent, Llandaff Cardiff, CF5 1 AR. Wales, U.K.
Beatrice Olbert & Josef Haenggi, Zak Zentrum fuer Agogik Gundeldingerstr. 173, CH-4053 Basel, Switzerland
Gisal Wnuk-Gette & Werner Wnuk, Dipl.Psych. D-88410 Bad Wurzach-Wengen 1, Germany
Rudolf Kronbichler, Family Therapist, LNK Salzburg, Abt. Jugendpsychiatrie Ignaz-Haarerstr. 79, A-5020 Salzburg, Austria
Matteo Selvini, PhD, Nuovo Centro per lo Studio della Famiglia 12, Viale Vittorio Veneto, I-20124 Milano, Italy
Gunthard Weber, MD, Heidelberger Institut fuer systemische Forschung/Therapie/Beratung, Kussmaulstrasse 10, D-69120 Heidelberg, Germany

REFERENCES

Hare-Mustin, R.E. & Marecek, J. (1990). *Making a Difference: Psychology and the Construction of Gender.* New Haven, CT: Yale University Press.
Hildenbrand, B. (in press). (Familien)-Therapie und Politik: Folgerungen aus dem Meilener Konzept therapeutischen Wissens und Handelns zur Abgrenzung und Verschraenkung beider Sphaeren, *Journal "Kontexte."* Freiburg i.B.
Hildenbrand, B. & Welter-Enderlin, R. (in press). Systemic Therapy as an Emotional Encounter, "Meilen-Concept." Stuttgart: Klett-Cotta.
Hoffman, E. (1993). *Exit into History.* New York: Penguin Books.
Imber-Black, E., Roberts, J. & Whiting, R. (1988). *Rituals in Families and Family Therapy.* New York: Norton.
Rambo, A.H., Heath, A. & Chenail, R.H. (1993). *Practicing Therapy.* New York: Norton.
Sheinberg, M. & Penn, P. (1991). Gender Dilemmas, Gender Questions and the Gender Mantra. *Journal of Marital and Family Therapy,* 17, 33-44.
Tomm, K. (July 1994, unpublished). Internalized Other Interviewing. University of Calgary.
Welter-Enderlin, R. (1987). Familismus, Sexismus und Familientherapie. *Familiendynamik Journal,* 12.
Welter-Enderlin, R. (1992). *Paare–Leidenschaft und lange Weile (Couples: Passion and Compassion).* Munich: Piper.
White, M. (1992). Men's Culture, the Men's Movement & the Constitution of Men's Lives. *Dulwich Center Newsletter,* No. 3 & 4.

Feminist-Informed Training
in Family Therapy:
Approaching the Millenium

Judith Myers Avis

SUMMARY. This paper explores the history and present state of development of feminist training in family therapy, from the perspective of the author's personal experience. It also suggests future directions for expanding feminist-informed training and for giving it a
more central and integrated place in our curricula. *[Article copies
available from The Haworth Document Delivery Service: 1-800-342-9678.
E-mail address: getinfo@haworth.com]*

I am grateful for this opportunity to reflect on a subject that has
been at the heart of my professional work for the better part of two
decades. Since 1977, before the term "feminist family therapy"
existed, I have been searching for ways to integrate a feminist
understanding into both my clinical practice and my work as an
educator, trainer, and supervisor of therapists. As I write these
words, I feel old! I also feel encouraged that the feminist perspectives on training that many of us fought simply to have named and
acknowledged 18 years ago are, today, the subject of legitimate
study and theorizing internationally, as well as the focus of this
volume devoted to feminist perspectives in our field. We have,

Judith Myers Avis, PhD, is Professor in the Marriage and Family Therapy
Program at the University of Guelph, Guelph, Ontario, Canada, N1G 2W1.

[Haworth co-indexing entry note]: "Feminist-Informed Training in Family Therapy: Approaching
the Millenium." Avis, Judith Myers. Co-published simultaneously in *Journal of Feminist Family Therapy* (The Haworth Press, Inc.) Vol. 8, No. 2, 1996, pp. 75-83; and: *Reflections on Feminist Family
Therapy Training* (ed: Kathy Weingarten, and Michele Bograd) The Haworth Press, Inc., 1996, pp. 75-83.
Single or multiple copies of this article are available from The Haworth Document Delivery Service
[1-800-342-9678, 9:00 a.m. - 5:00 p.m. (EST). E-mail address: getinfo@haworth.com].

indeed, come a long way!–from the total absence of theorizing about gender in family therapy prior to Rachel Hare-Mustin's pioneering article in 1978, to a fairly wide recognition, in 1996, of gender as a fundamental category of social organization and clinical theorizing. We have, however, much further to go. As a field, we still lack consensus about why gender is important, about how to think about it clinically, or about how to address it in practice or training.

The articles in this collection demonstrate family therapy's increasing attention to gender by depicting training programs in both North America and Europe which intentionally integrate a feminist perspective into many or all aspects of their teaching. These articles provide a snapshot of the current state of feminist-informed training. They highlight its advanced development in some contexts and its continued absence in others; the growing impact of social constructionist and narrative ideas; the richness and convergence of teaching and supervision techniques developed in differing national contexts; and the growing awareness of the intersection of gender with other categories of oppression, such as race, class, culture, and sexual orientation. They also demonstrate our growing recognition that just as there are many "feminisms," there are many feminist approaches to therapy and training.

To place today's developments in feminist-informed training into historical perspective, I would like to reflect on my own journey over the past 19 years, which has been driven by my professional mission both to integrate a feminist consciousness into my work as a family therapy educator, and to persuade the field to incorporate gender analysis into its theory, practice, and training. When I was first attracted to family therapy in the mid-seventies, I was surprised and dismayed to discover the field's obliviousness to gender and its commitment to sexist, woman-blaming theories and practices. Like Cheryl Rampage (this volume), I experienced years of feeling split between my family systems self and my feminist self, and of struggling to integrate these two seemingly incompatible perspectives. At the time, I was teaching in a social work program in a small Catholic university in eastern Canada.

In 1982 I proposed a new, feminist course on social work with women, which included a section on feminist counseling. The reaction to this course proposal was sharp and defensive, but not surprising, given the context. The all-male curriculum committee challenged the course as political rather than academic, because the course outline openly stated that it began with the assumption of women's oppression. The course was reluctantly approved despite many protests, and was a powerful turning point in my own development of consciousness, as well as that of the students. I learned about the power of ideas to transform and to politicize, as the women saw their lives reflected in the literature in a way they had not experienced before, and the men felt challenged in their privilege.

I also experienced for the first time what Cheryl Rampage refers to as the system's power to silence. As word about the course spread beyond the borders of the classroom, several male colleagues from other departments, friends in earlier days, simply stopped speaking to me. The wife of one of them was a student in the course and she reported that one day her husband scooped up her course books and reported that he was going to show the president (a Catholic Monsignor) just what kind of garbage we were reading "in that damned course"! I experienced the loss of my safe position as a nonthreatening and respected colleague as extremely painful and anxiety-provoking. I vividly remember feeling that I was out alone on a limb that was about to be sawed off. Fortunately, there were many affirming outcomes which made the emotional costs seem less significant. The 20 women and 5 men students were adamant in their declarations that this had been the most important course in their professional training and that they could not imagine practicing social work without it. After its conclusion, they successfully petitioned the department to have it made a permanent and required part of the curriculum.

This introduction to developing feminist-informed training became a significant turning point for me in refocusing my professional direction. I decided that if I wanted to have a voice which could not easily be silenced, it would help to have a Ph.D. From 1983 to 1986, while I was a student in the Purdue doctoral program (which was considered one of the top in the country), issues of gender, power, violence, control, and sexual abuse were mainly absent from the curriculum, and peripheral when addressed at all.

My feminist sister students and I made it our business to raise these subjects at every opportunity, not always endearing ourselves to our faculty or fellow students, yet clearly making a difference in consciousness for some. Concerned about the lack of gender content in our own training, we wrote about how family therapy could be reconceptualized and how training could be expanded (Avis, 1986; Wheeler, 1985).

After completing my doctorate, I joined the faculty of the master's program in Marriage and Family Therapy at the University of Guelph. As the first and only woman teaching in the program, I was regarded with both hope and suspicion by the students. I experienced the weight of expectation of many women students to be the role model they had previously missed, to take stands on gender issues whenever they arose, to be always wise and fair, to understand them, and to have answers. For the three male students in the program, my arrival posed a great challenge. They were suddenly in the unexpected situation of having a woman professor requiring them to read literature written by women from women's perspectives. As one of the men later commented to me, this experience was extremely personally unbalancing, challenging as it did the usual organization of power in the program, the university, and the field. I learned from him just how threatening such a reversal can be, with its experience of sudden unseating from an assumed position of privilege.

In my early years of teaching in this program, I experienced both resistance and relief from students when I introduced gender issues into the curriculum. I also experienced both the loneliness and the sense of responsibility of being the only woman and the only feminist on faculty. I struggled with many things: with isolation and the absence of feminist family therapists with whom to collaborate in the university; with fear of being rejected, not liked, categorized, seen as anti-male or male bashing if I presented feminist ideas or asked hard questions about gender or power; with the anger of some students. One year, my office door was, overnight, pointedly denuded of all its gender-related news clippings. I also struggled with finding and maintaining my voice—a task that still seems formidable at times.

At the present time, I have the opportunity to integrate feminist ideas into my teaching and supervision in program-sanctioned ways that I would not have believed possible in 1978. I teach a practicum embedded in both feminist and narrative ideas, a theory course that integrates feminist perspectives into all parts of the course, and includes several sessions focussed specifically on feminist approaches to family therapy, and a course on working with violence and abuse in families. The fact that all of these courses are required as part of the core curriculum, carries a message about their legitimacy and importance. I now have colleagues who emphasize social justice, diversity, and feminist social constructionist perspectives in their teaching, supervision, training, and research. Working with colleagues who share a political consciousness, although we often differ significantly in our particular understandings, is a joy after the isolation of earlier years.

Over these years of working to have feminist perspectives recognized in our field, I have, like others, both in this volume and in other parts of the world, faced a variety of challenges and struggles as well as joys. I have come to think of these challenges as an apparently necessary part of introducing feminist content into a field so long blind to these issues. In the following paragraphs, I will share some of these experiences in the hope of encouraging those who toil in similar ground, and in the belief that sharing is the best antidote to oppression.

N. Norma Akamatsu, Kathryn Basham, and Mary Olson refer to Foucault's description of feminism as "the insurrection of subjugated knowledge." This aptly describes the theme of both my personal and professional journeys—one of discovering my own subjugated knowledge and finding my voice to express it. Beginning with my experience of a dominating and controlling father who forbade either knowledge or voice different from his own, I learned discretion and indirect assertion for survival. My professional life reproduced this experience as I learned that women's voices were generally devalued and, when challenging patriarchy, silenced. Cheryl Rampage, Pilar Hernandez, and Rosmarie Welter-Enderlin all refer to their own experiences of being silenced. The tension between finding my voice and maintaining the courage to express it has been a major theme of my professional life. Each time I have found my voice, I have experienced a release of energy and personal agency which has been personally empowering. At the same time, I have also experienced the pain and the fear of the backlash–of being dismissed, ignored, silently disapproved, misunderstood, misrepresented, labelled, categorized, and marginalized. As I have experienced the power of the system to intimidate and silence, I have struggled to continue finding my courage and my voice in the face of it.

I try not to take the backlash personally. In 1991, I was part of a plenary presentation at the annual meeting of the American Family Therapy Academy regarding family therapists' lack of response to violence and abuse in families (Avis, 1992). The volatile audience response suggested I had crossed some unspoken line whereby dominant practices and thinking were not to be questioned. Hours after my plenary I was verbally accosted by a male colleague, so furious with me that I thought for a moment I might be in some danger–a fear shared by several colleagues who were with me at the time. Subsequently, in professional journals and meetings, an inordinate amount of airtime and space has been taken by the small percentage of people who did not like the plenary (15-20%, according to the evaluations), who have rewritten history. Those who thought the plenary was outstanding did not receive the same public hearing.

Michael White once asked me if I was not being a bit naive to think that I could challenge the tactics of oppression and not expect to have those same tactics then used against me. I remind myself of his question. I attempt to keep perspective, to remember how far we have come without losing sight of how far we have yet to go, and to remind myself that at the end of the day I must be able to live with myself and the choices I have made. It helps to share the struggles with like-minded colleagues, both in my own context and around the world. And it helps to keep my focus on the positive: to remember the distance travelled; to see students become alive and empowered as they develop a perspective on gender in which they can locate themselves; to recognize that I have, in a small way, been able to make a difference; to realize that I do not have to do it all, or do it all myself; to confront my own limitations, errors, and areas of blindness with compassion and self-acceptance; to look at the world from a postmodern perspective and examine my own ideas from a position of non-defensive self-reflexivity; to remember the power of laughter and humor; and to maintain balance in my life and in my work.

I have also been challenged by feelings of guilt as I have confronted my own areas of privilege and blindness and the potential oppressiveness of some of my ideas and practices. It has been humbling, for example, and often painful, to look honestly at the oppressive impact of globalizing ideas or the power of language to reduce persons to one dimension–as men, women, perpetrators, victims, etc., as well as to become more conscious of my blind participation in white, middle-class, affluent, able-bodied, heterosexual dominance.

What, then, of the future? Here are a few thoughts. I would suggest that the future of feminist-informed family therapy training lies in making connections–between gender and other forms of oppression; between violence and injustice; between men and women; between gender, power, and clinical practice; and between power relations at personal and global levels. Not only is the personal political: it is a reflection of the relations of power nationally, internationally, and globally–relations which involve the domination and rape of the environment, the land, nations, and peoples, as well as of women. It has been suggested that we may only have 15 years left to save the planet. This possibility puts our efforts into a wider perspective. They become part of a larger movement to transform all human relationships so they are based on principles of social justice. Without such transformation, without finding ways to co-habit this earth without exploiting or oppressing others, or the planet itself, we will surely destroy ourselves. I believe that as we train therapists to help couples and families free themselves from oppressive relationships, we are actually helping to build the foundations and the will at the local level for global transformation.

To these ends, I believe men and women in family therapy must become equally engaged in efforts to understand and challenge oppression in all its forms. This includes the necessity for men to join with women and women to join with men, both in expanding our thinking about gender and in training our students to expand theirs. This is not gender-specific work, although it has been undertaken primarily by women up to this time. Women cannot do it alone. These issues are of too great fundamental importance to all of us, as Matteo Selvini's words, reported by Rosmarie Welter-Enderlin, attest. It further includes expanding our understanding of the ways in which many men's lives, as well as women's, have been constricted by violence, control, and socialization, and integrating this understanding into our theory and practice. As we understand more about the impact on men's consciousness of the excesses of "normal" male socialization, of physical discipline and abuse, and of being trained for and sent to war, I believe we will expand both our compassion and our options for helping men to take their lives back from traditional masculinity. I would like to see feminist-informed training in family therapy seek ways to connect with men's pain as well as with women's, being careful not to regard such pain as an excuse for violence or the misuse of power. If we are going to promote change in the lives of families, we must find effective ways to help men, as well as women, to change.

I agree with Pilar Hernandez that it is essential that we develop theoretical, clinical, training, and political initiatives to address the interaction of gender with other forms of oppression. One challenge as we expand our understanding of the complex interaction of privilege, dominance, and oppression may be to keep gender central, and not peripheral, in the discourse. Without such centrality, I fear it may be all too easy to refocus on other forms of oppression and put women's experience, yet again, aside. In this work, I believe narrative ideas have particular potential for expanding our future thinking about the construction of gender and oppressive relationships, as well as about how to actualize feminist-informed practice and training.

I would suggest that our future efforts must integrate a feminist analysis of gender, power, and oppression at two different levels in training. The first offers breadth by integrating this analysis into all aspects of training and supervision, into every class and every case discussion, as N. Norma Akamatsu and her colleagues point out. The second level involves specific courses, required and in the core curriculum, where the issues can be explored in greater depth. Courses on gender issues, diversity, and working with violence are examples. As long as such courses are optional rather than part of the core curriculum, the analysis of gender relations will be marginalized and regarded as a special interest rather than as fundamental to ethical practice.

Finally, as we move towards the millennium, I find myself thinking a lot about balance. I am concerned about living in greater balance and harmony at all levels of my life: physical, intellectual, spiritual, and emotional. I seek to balance my commitment to external, political work with my commitment to internal work. I agree with Cheryl Rampage about the importance of teaching by example, of modelling what we teach. When I overwork, I buy into the oppressive model of work, success, and productivity espoused by patriarchy. When I take time for myself and for self-care, set boundaries, let go, and refuse to be any longer co-opted into the dominant career model of overwork and burnout, I give my students permission to make similar choices. I have been surprised at how direct the translation is. When I overwork, I make greater demands on students as well as on myself and we all suffer from burnout. When I am less demanding and live more in balance, so do my students. Perhaps, as we confront the challenges of the coming years both locally and globally, some of the greatest challenges of feminist family therapy training will be in accepting that no one of us can do it all, in promoting loving, respectful, nonexploitative relationships with ourselves, the planet, and with those around us, and in teaching our trainees to do likewise.

REFERENCES

Avis, J.M. (1986). Training and supervision in feminist-informed family therapy: A Delphi study. Unpublished doctoral dissertation. Purdue University.

Avis, J.M. (1992). Violence and abuse in families: The problem and family therapy's response. *Journal of Marital and Family Therapy, 18*, 223-230.

Hare-Mustin, R. (1978). A feminist approach to family therapy. *Family Process, 17*, 181-194.

Wheeler, D. (1985). The theory and practice of feminist-informed family therapy: A Delphi study. Unpublished doctoral dissertation. Purdue University.

Index

Haworth
DOCUMENT DELIVERY
SERVICE

This valuable service provides a single-article order form for any article from a Haworth journal.

- *Time Saving:* No running around from library to library to find a specific article.
- *Cost Effective:* All costs are kept down to a minimum.
- *Fast Delivery:* Choose from several options, including same-day FAX.
- *No Copyright Hassles:* You will be supplied by the original publisher.
- *Easy Payment:* Choose from several easy payment methods.

Open Accounts Welcome for . . .
- Library Interlibrary Loan Departments
- Library Network/Consortia Wishing to Provide Single-Article Services
- Indexing/Abstracting Services with Single Article Provision Services
- Document Provision Brokers and Freelance Information Service Providers

---

MAIL or FAX THIS ENTIRE ORDER FORM TO:

Haworth Document Delivery Service
The Haworth Press, Inc.
10 Alice Street
Binghamton, NY 13904-1580

or FAX: 1-800-895-0582
or CALL: 1-800-342-9678
9am-5pm EST

PLEASE SEND ME PHOTOCOPIES OF THE FOLLOWING SINGLE ARTICLES:

1) Journal Title: _____
   Vol/Issue/Year: _____ Starting & Ending Pages: _____
   Article Title: _____

2) Journal Title: _____
   Vol/Issue/Year: _____ Starting & Ending Pages: _____
   Article Title: _____

3) Journal Title: _____
   Vol/Issue/Year: _____ Starting & Ending Pages: _____
   Article Title: _____

4) Journal Title: _____
   Vol/Issue/Year: _____ Starting & Ending Pages: _____
   Article Title: _____

(See other side for Costs and Payment Information)

COSTS: Please figure your cost to order quality copies of an article.

1. Set-up charge per article: $8.00
   ($8.00 × number of separate articles) _____

2. Photocopying charge for each article:

   1-10 pages: $1.00 _____

   11-19 pages: $3.00 _____

   20-29 pages: $5.00 _____

   30+ pages: $2.00/10 pages _____

3. Flexicover (optional): $2.00/article _____

4. Postage & Handling: US: $1.00 for the first article/

   $.50 each additional article _____

   Federal Express: $25.00 _____

   Outside US: $2.00 for first article/
   $.50 each additional article_____

5. Same-day FAX service: $.35 per page _____

GRAND TOTAL: _____

METHOD OF PAYMENT: (please check one)

❑ Check enclosed   ❑ Please ship and bill. PO # _____
(sorry we can ship and bill to bookstores only! All others must pre-pay)

❑ Charge to my credit card: ❑ Visa; ❑ MasterCard; ❑ Discover;
❑ American Express;

Account Number:_____ Expiration date:_____

Signature: *X*_____

Name: _____ Institution: _____

Address: _____

_____

City: _____ State:_____ Zip:_____

Phone Number: _____ FAX Number: _____

MAIL or *FAX* THIS ENTIRE ORDER FORM TO:

Haworth Document Delivery Service	**or FAX:** 1-800-895-0582
The Haworth Press, Inc.	**or CALL:** 1-800-342-9678
10 Alice Street	9am-5pm EST)
Binghamton, NY 13904-1580	